CRICUT® SURVIVAL GUIDE

the practical, problem-first companion for crafters

BY

JENNIFERMAKER

ABOUT THIS SURVIVAL GUIDE

This Survival Guide is a **practical, problem-first companion** for crafters who want clear answers without overwhelm. It's designed to be skimmable, searchable, and focused on what to try first when things go wrong – from Design Space issues to cutting, materials, and "Print Then Cut" problems.

This isn't a technical manual or a feature tour. It's a confidence-building guide built on one simple truth: you're not bad at Cricut, and troubleshooting is part of crafting. By the end, you'll know **how to fix common issues quickly** – and when to stop – so you can get back to making what you love.

Hi! I'm Jennifer!

Each section walks you through the most common causes first, with clear explanations of why a problem happens and what actually fixes it, rather than just a long list of settings to change. You'll learn how to recognize the difference between a quick fix and a time-sink, avoid the most common mistakes, and feel more confident making adjustments on your own. This guide respects your time, your materials, and your creativity.

If you have any questions about using this Survival Guide, email me at hello@jennifermaker.com. For Cricut ideas and inspiration, join me at https://jennifermaker.com/cricutcrafters.

Happy making,

Jennifer

Version 1.0 – Print Edition – Published February 2026 – JenniferMaker® LLC

FIND WHAT YOU NEED

This Guide Contents helps you quickly find exactly what you're looking for in the Survival Guide. Just flip to the section you need and dive in!

(Table of Contents continued on next page)

FIND WHAT YOU NEED (CONTINUED)

HOW TO USE THIS SURVIVAL GUIDE

Welcome to the Cricut Survival Guide!

If you're holding this book, take a deep breath, because you're in the right place, regardless of which Cricut cutting machine(s) you own. This guide is designed to be used, not read cover to cover like a novel. It's skimmable, searchable, and **built around real problems you're actually experiencing.** It's not a tour of every button Cricut has ever added or moved. You won't find long-winded explanations or a bunch of technical jargon here.

Instead, you'll see **clear "try this first" steps** that help you get unstuck fast, whether your machine won't cut, Cricut Design Space won't open, or your vinyl just will not behave. Picture me sitting next to you saying, "Okay, let's fix this together!"

Here's what this guide isn't: it's not a replacement for Cricut manuals, and it's **not meant to overwhelm you** with every possible setting.

What it IS: a problem-first survival guide. If something goes wrong, you flip to the section that matches the frustration you're having, and you start there. Each section is written so you can quickly scan the bolded issues, find the one that sounds like your problem, and follow a logical path forward without guessing. **Minimal fluff, maximum clarity** – because when you're crafting, time and patience are precious.

THE CRICUT MINDSET

Let's talk about the biggest shift that will change everything: the Cricut mindset. Most Cricut issues are not because you're bad at crafting, not tech-savvy enough, or "doing it wrong." Cricut problems usually fall into three buckets: software issues (Design Space), machine issues (the Cricut machines themselves), or material issues (what you're crafting with). Once you understand which bucket you're dealing with, troubleshooting becomes dramatically easier and way less frustratingly stressful. A Design Space crash is not the same kind of problem as a blade tearing cardstock, and treating them the same will only make you more frustrated.

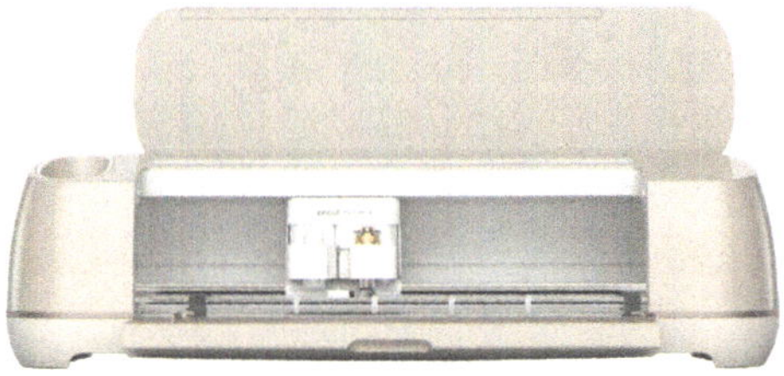

This is where the 80/20 rule of Cricut troubleshooting comes in, and it's a game changer. **About 80% of Cricut problems come from the same 20% of causes:** incorrect settings, recent updates, file prep mistakes, or material setup issues. That's why this book focuses so heavily on those areas. Before you assume your machine is broken, we'll walk through Design Space glitches, cutting problems, material-specific fixes, and common user mistakes that everyone makes ... yes, even experienced crafters like me!

Most of the time, **the fix is simpler than it feels** once you know where to look. As you move through the book, you'll notice each section is organized around the way problems actually show up in real life. Design Space not opening? Missing buttons that don't match the tutorial? Cuts that are off, messy, or not cutting through? Materials that curl, tear, or refuse to stick? "Print Then Cut" behaving like it has a mind of its own? This guide meets you exactly at that moment of frustration and gives you a clear next step, and then another, if needed.

And finally, I want you to hear this clearly: you are not bad at crafting with a Cricut. Troubleshooting is part of crafting, not a failure of it. Every confident Cricut user you admire has been stuck, confused, and convinced their machine hated them at least once. Confidence doesn't come from never having problems. It comes from knowing what to try next. By the time you reach the end of this survival guide, you'll have something even better than perfect cuts: the confidence to fix issues calmly, quickly, and without panic. And that, my friend, is what keeps crafting fun.

WHAT KIND OF CRICUT PROBLEM ARE YOU HAVING?

Start here to find the right section fast.

Does Cricut Design Space open and work the way you expect?
- Yes
- No → Go to "Cricut Design Space Issues"

Is your Cricut machine failing to connect, start, or behave normally?
- Yes → Go to "Cutting Problems"
- No

Is the machine cutting, but the results are wrong or messy?
- Yes → Go to "Cutting Problems"
- No

Is the issue related to the material you're using?
- Yes → Go to "Material-Specific Troubleshooting"
- No

Are you trying to use Print Then Cut?
- Yes → Go to "Print Then Cut Survival"
- No

Could the problem be your mat, blade, or tool?
- Yes → Go to "Mats, Blades, and Tools"
- No

Could this be a setup or canvas mistake?
- Yes → Go to "Common User Mistakes"
- No

Have you tried everything and it still isn't working?
- Yes → Go to "Reset, Reboot, Recover"
- No

You're back on track! Have fun and create something!

TOP 20 CRICUT FIXES AT A GLANCE

DESIGN SPACE FIXES

1. RESTART DESIGN SPACE: Close the app completely and reopen it before trying anything else. It sounds simple, but this fixes a lot of little glitches.
2. CHECK FOR UPDATES: Missing buttons or strange behavior often mean an update is waiting.
3. LOG OUT AND LOG BACK IN: Great for missing projects, sync issues, or Cricut Access weirdness.
4. CLEAR CACHE: Especially helpful for freezing, lag, or blank screens.
5. SWITCH DEVICES: Some features work best (or only!) on desktop instead of mobile devices.

CUTTING & MACHINE FIXES

6. POWER CYCLE THE MACHINE: Turn off the machine, unplug it, wait 60 seconds, then plug it in and turn it back on.
7. CHECK YOUR CONNECTION: If Bluetooth is acting up, USB can be a lifesaver.
8. CONFIRM THE SELECTED MACHINE: This fixes a surprising number of cutting issues.
9. DOUBLE-CHECK THE TOOL AND CLAMP: Be sure the right tool is in the right clamp and seated properly.
10. UNLOAD AND RELOAD THE MAT: A slightly crooked mat can throw off the whole cut.

MATERIALS, MATS, & TOOLS FIXES

11. USE THE CORRECT MAT FOR THE MATERIAL: Mats that are too sticky or not sticky enough cause most material problems.
12. CLEAN OR REPLACE THE BLADE: Use an alcohol wipe to clean the blade, or if problems persist, replace the blade.
13. ADJUST PRESSURE: Increase or decrease the pressure if your cuts are not clean.
14. TEST CUT FIRST: A small test cut saves a full sheet of wasted material.
15. SECURE MATERIALS: Use a brayer to secure the material or tape the edges when needed.

PROJECT SETUP FIXES

16. CHECK YOUR LAYERS PANEL: Many problems can be found here, especially for Print Then Cut.
17. CONFIRM ATTACH VS FLATTEN VS GROUP: One click can change how the project cuts.
18. VERIFY CANVAS UNITS: If everything is the wrong size, verify that the canvas is set to the correct units (inches vs mm).
19. MIRROR IRON-ON BEFORE CUTTING: Yes, even seasoned makers forget this sometimes.
20. REINSTALL: When all else fails, uninstall and reinstall Design Space.

CRICUT DESIGN SPACE ISSUES

- Freezing on Load
- White Screen or Blank Canvas
- Mobile vs. Desktop Differences
- My Screen Doesn't Look Like the Tutorial
- Features Moved or Renamed
- Beta vs. Live Features
- Updates and Rollbacks
- SVG Won't Upload
- PNG Uploads as a Cut File Instead of Print Then Cut
- Some Layers are Merged or Missing
- "Upload Failed" Errors
- Projects Are Not Saving
- Projects Are Missing
- Offline vs. Cloud Confusion
- Account Sync Problems

FREEZE ON LOADING

Is Cricut Design Space freezing when you open it so that you can't access projects, upload files, create designs, or even click on anything? This can be very frustrating, but there's usually a quick and simple solution.

1

WAIT ONE FULL MINUTE: The initial sync can look frozen, but it may still be loading. Walk away, get a cup of tea, and come back – things are probably ready to go!

2

CHECK INTERNET STRENGTH: Cricut Design Space needs an internet connection unless you've switched to Offline mode. So if your network strength is weak, switch networks if possible.

3

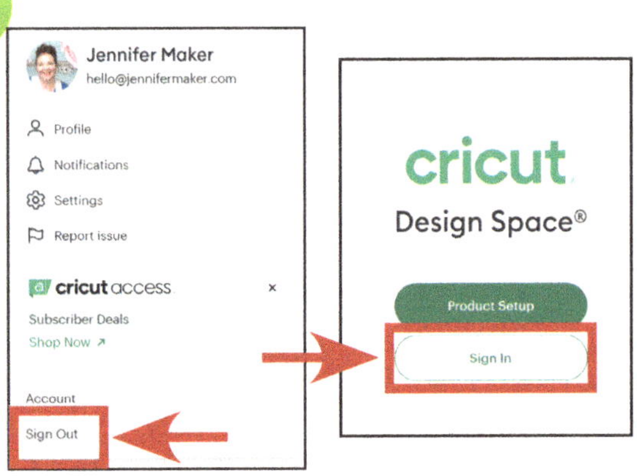

LOG OUT, THEN BACK IN: Log out of your Cricut account (click on your name, then click "Sign Out"), then log back in. This forces a fresh account sync.

4

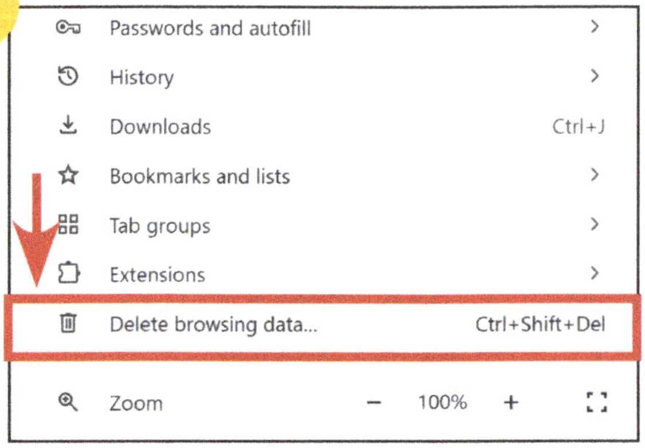

CLEAR YOUR CACHE (DESKTOP ONLY): If you're on a computer, clear your Internet cache, then reinstall Design Space. Reinstalling fixes most load freezes.

WHITE SCREEN OR BLANK CANVAS

Did Cricut Design Space start up, but you only have a blank white screen or canvas, as if the program didn't finish fully loading? Here's how to solve this issue.

1

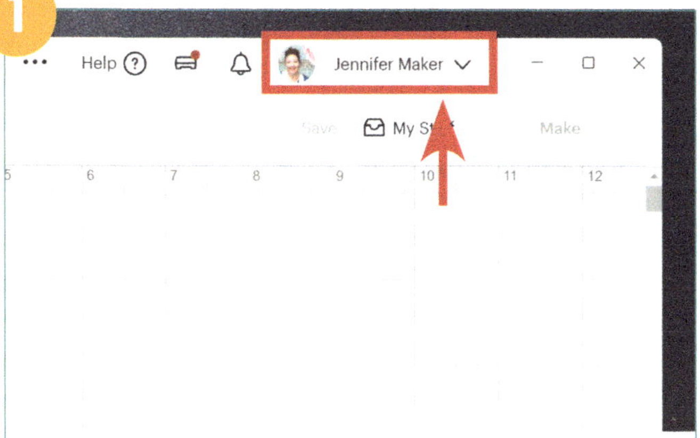

ENSURE THAT YOU'RE LOGGED IN: White screens can mean a login failure, so ensure that you are logged in to your Cricut account. Your name and profile picture (if you have one set) should be in the top right corner of the window.

2

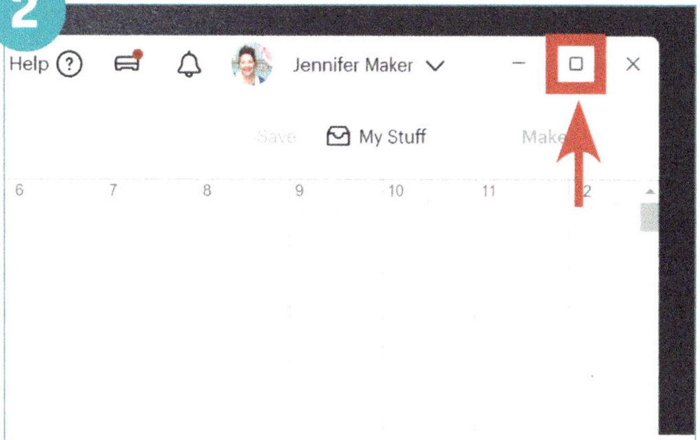

RESIZE THE APP WINDOW: The Design Space Canvas sometimes loads off-screen, so try resizing the window to fill your screen.

3

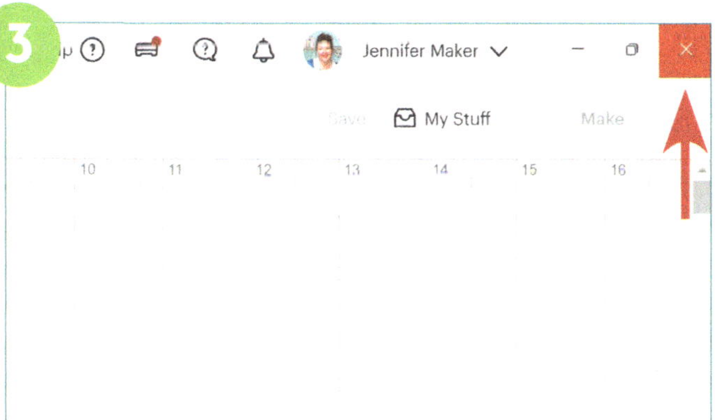

RESTART DESIGN SPACE: Close out of Cricut Design Space entirely, then restart the program. On a Windows PC, click the "X" in the upper right corner. On a Mac, go to the Cricut Design Space menu in the upper left corner and choose Quit.

4

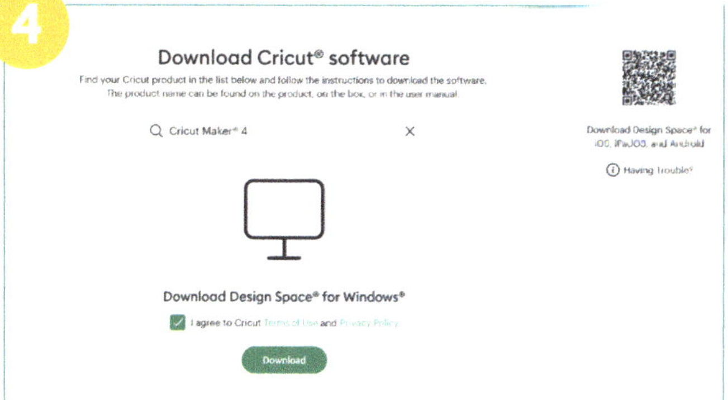

REINSTALL DESIGN SPACE: If you're still having problems, uninstall Design Space, then redownload and reinstall it by going to design.cricut.com.

MOBILE VS DESKTOP DIFFERENCES

Although it's the same program, there are some differences between the Desktop and mobile (iOS, Android) versions of Design Space. If you're having issues with the mobile version, try these solutions.

1

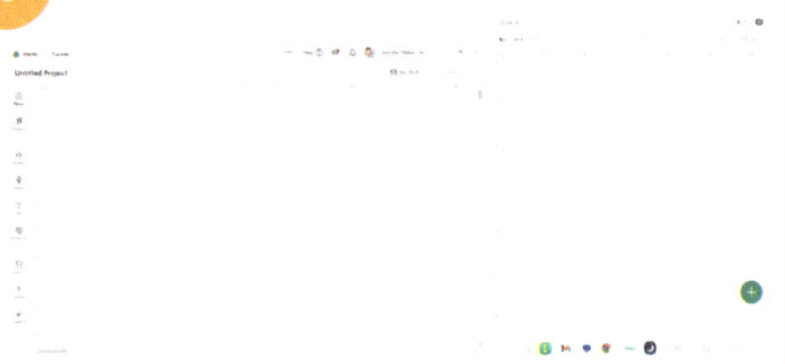

DESKTOP MOBILE

MANY TUTORIALS USE DESKTOP: The Desktop version and the mobile versions don't look the same, so it's important to know which platform the tutorial is using and adjust accordingly if you're not using the same platform.

2

DESKTOP MOBILE

LOOK FOR MOBILE-ONLY LIMITS: Some tasks require the Desktop version of Design Space and cannot be done in the mobile version of the program. For example, you cannot work in Offline mode on an Android device.

3

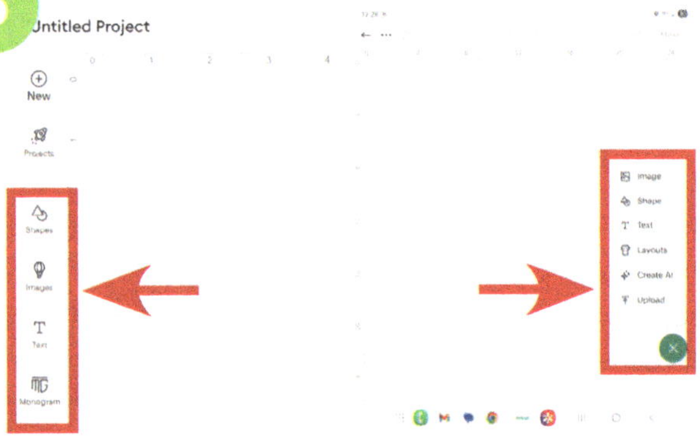

CHECK FEATURE LOCATION CHANGES: Menu and tool locations differ between platforms, i.e. some tools are always visible on the left side of the Desktop version, whereas you must click the plus sign to access them in the mobile version.

4

SWITCH DEVICES IF NEEDED: Unless you're just cutting an already-completed project or working on something simple, it's usually easier to use Design Space to its full potential on a Desktop rather than on a mobile device.

MY SCREEN DOESN'T LOOK LIKE THE TUTORIAL

Are you trying to follow a Design Space tutorial, but your screen doesn't match the tutorial you're using? This can be really confusing, but there are some things you can do to help solve this problem.

1

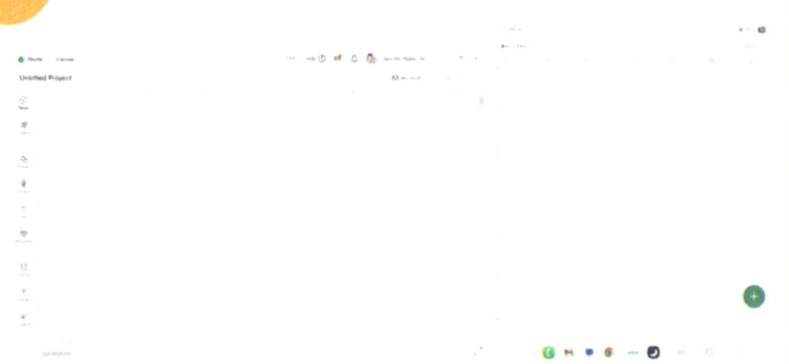

DESKTOP MOBILE

CONFIRM WHICH PLATFORM THE TUTORIAL USES: The Desktop version and the mobile versions don't look the same, so it's important to know which platform the tutorial is using and adjust accordingly if you're not using the same platform.

2

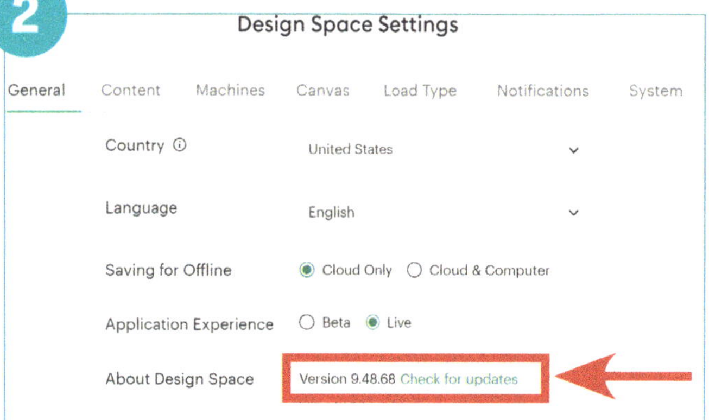

CHECK THE APP VERSION: The tutorial you are looking at may show older layouts, especially since Design Space updates frequently. To check your app version, click on your name at the top of the screen and click Settings.

3

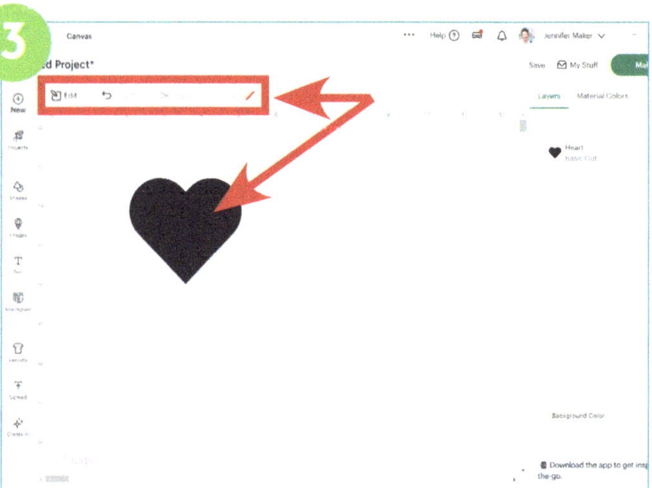

ADD AN OBJECT TO THE CANVAS: Most tools appear only when there is something on the Canvas.

4

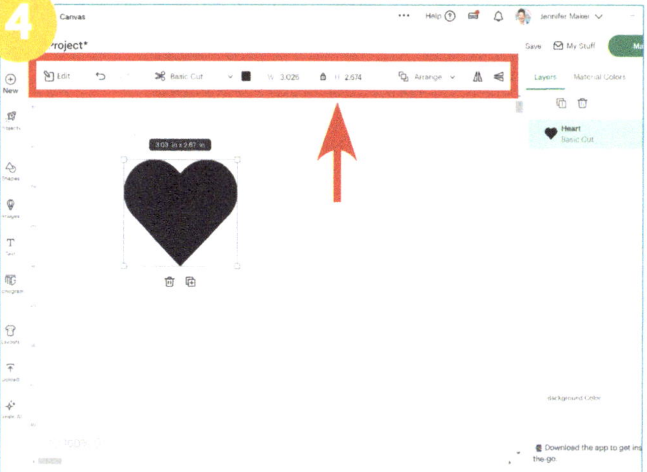

SELECT AN OBJECT: Most tools appear only when something on the Canvas is selected.

FEATURES MOVED OR RENAMED

Did you open Cricut Design Space and find that it doesn't look the same as it did when you were creating your last project? That probably means that Design Space has recently been updated.

1

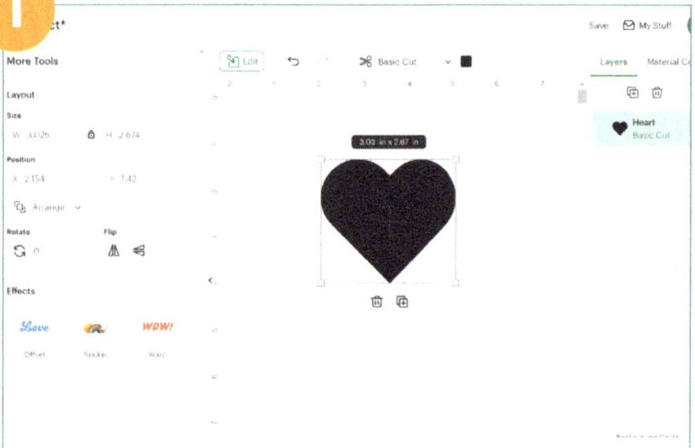

CHECK THE TOOLBAR: Many tools have been relocated with recent updates. You'll find that many features are now in the Edit menu, which opens when you click the pencil icon.

2

LOOK FOR ICON CHANGES: The same tool you've always used may have a new icon or symbol. It's also possible that the name may have changed, too. For example, "Layouts" has replaced "Templates."

3

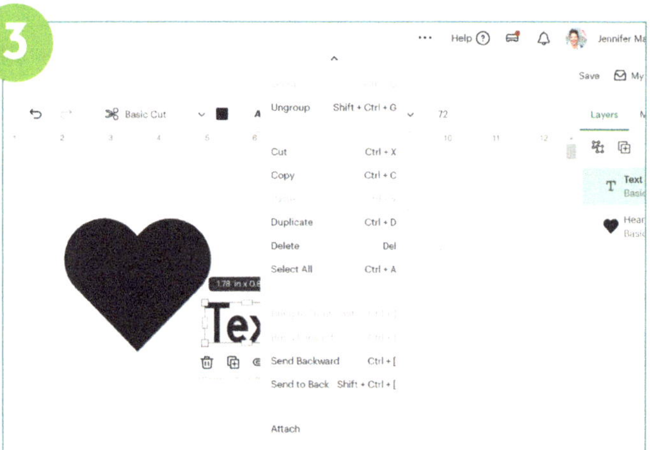

RIGHT-CLICK YOUR MOUSE ON THE CANVAS: Some features that used to have an icon now need you to select an object and click with your right mouse button to open a menu.

4

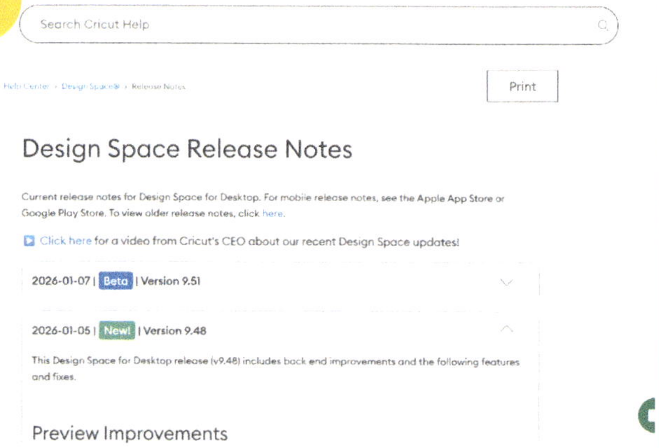

SEARCH CRICUT RELEASE NOTES: You can learn about and confirm changes by reading the release notes for recent updates at help.cricut.com.

BETA VS LIVE FEATURES

Did you know that there are two versions of Cricut Design Space? The Live version is the officially released version, while the Beta version is in a testing phase. You can work in either version by choosing it in the Settings menu.

1

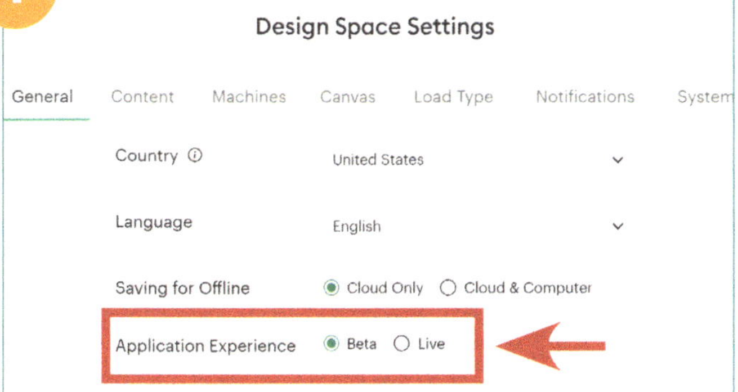

CHECK IF YOU'RE USING BETA: Cricut Design Space Beta version users see experimental layouts that haven't officially been rolled out. Click on your name at the top of the screen, click Settings, and General to view which app experience you are using.

2

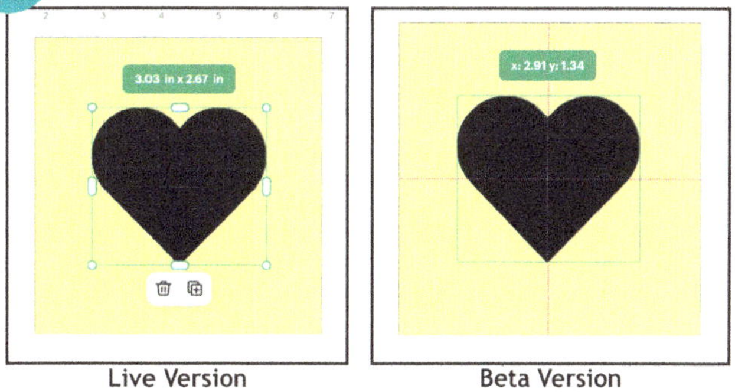

Live Version
No guidelines

Beta Version
New guidelines

COMPARE WITH THE LIVE VERSION: Tutorials usually show the Live version of Design Space, not the Beta version. For example, at the time of publishing this guide, you won't see placement guidelines in the Live version, but you will in the Beta version.

3

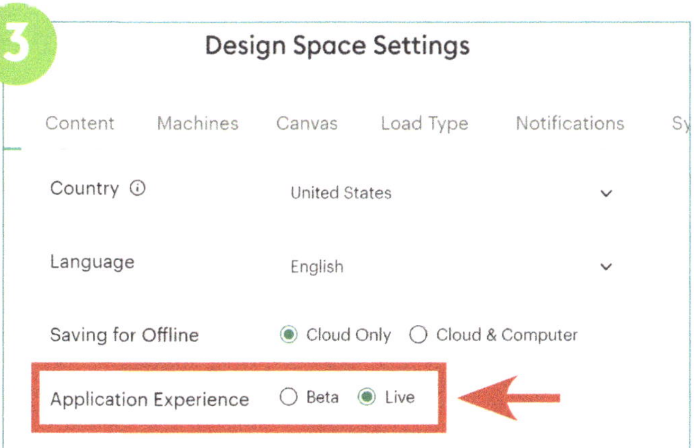

SWITCH VERSIONS AS NEEDED: If you're struggling, use the Live version, not Beta, to match up with tutorials. Switch versions in the Settings menu under "Application Experience." Design Space will close down and restart.

4

EXPECT SOME INSTABILITY: The Beta version sometimes experiences glitches and bugs. New tools and features may not be permanent and can disappear without warning, so be aware of this!

UPDATES AND ROLLBACKS

Cricut Design Space is frequently updated to add features, fix bugs and glitches, and improve your experience. Here's what to do if you see changes or are having issues with new changes.

1

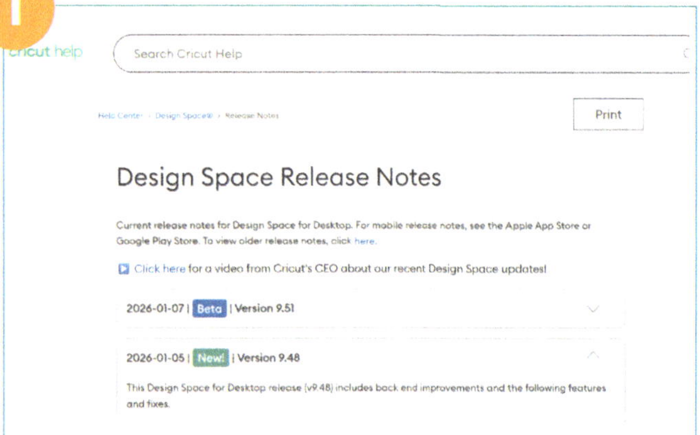

CHECK UPDATE HISTORY: A recent update may have changed tools, so look at the changes made in the most recent updates by checking the release notes at help.cricut.com.

2

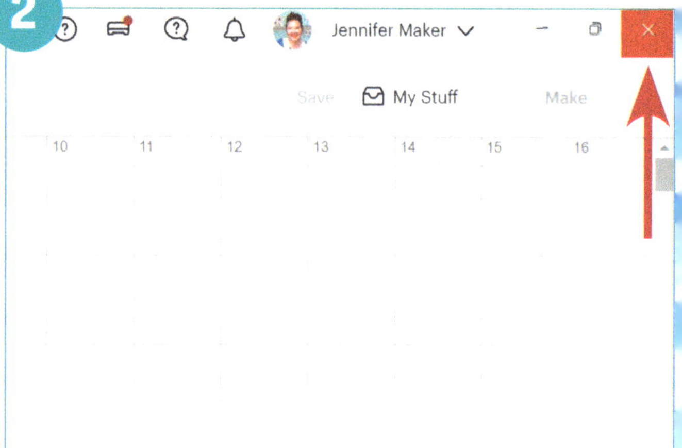

RESTART AFTER UPDATING: If you don't see new updates and you've already installed them, close out of the program entirely and restart Design Space.

3

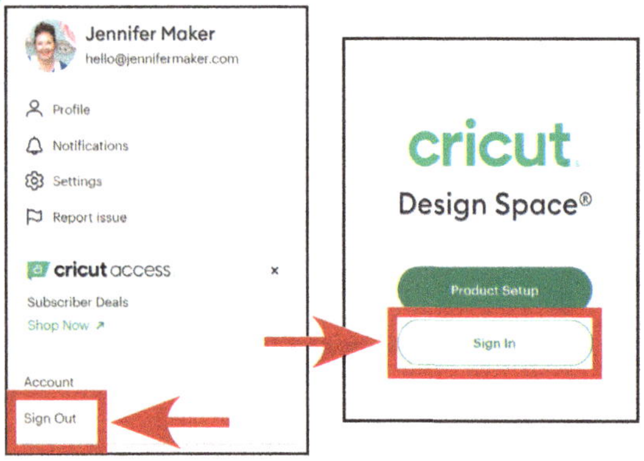

LOG OUT AND BACK IN: Log out and log back in to your Cricut account to refresh feature notifications, which is the little red circle with a number inside it at the top of the window.

4

WAIT 24-48 HOURS: Quick behind-the-scenes fixes are common after updates, so wait a day or two, then try again.

SVG WON'T UPLOAD

Are you having issues uploading an SVG file to Cricut Design Space? This can be very frustrating, so follow the information below to solve it!

1

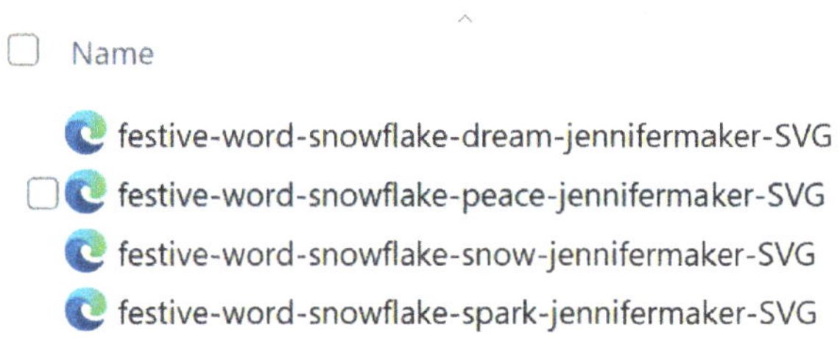

CONFIRM THE FILE IS TRULY AN SVG: Some files are mislabeled, so check the file type. It should end in ".svg" or appear as a "Microsoft Edge HTML Document." Also, ensure that the file has been extracted if it was downloaded in a Zip file.

2

GIVE IT TIME: A large file may take a little longer to fully upload, so give it a little extra time.

3

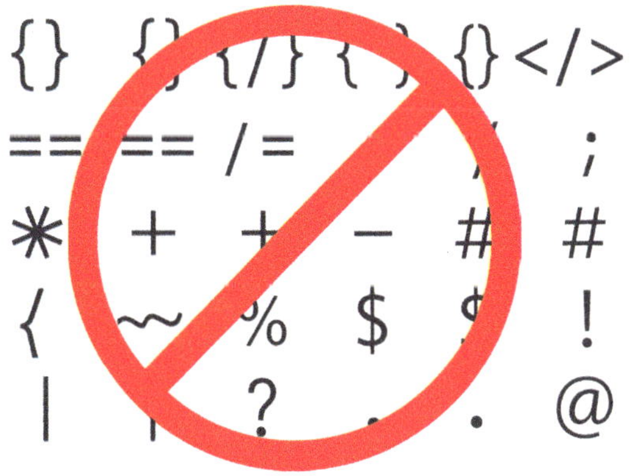

RENAME THE FILE: Avoid special characters, which are characters other than letters and numbers. Special characters can cause errors, compatibility issues, and misinterpreted commands.

4

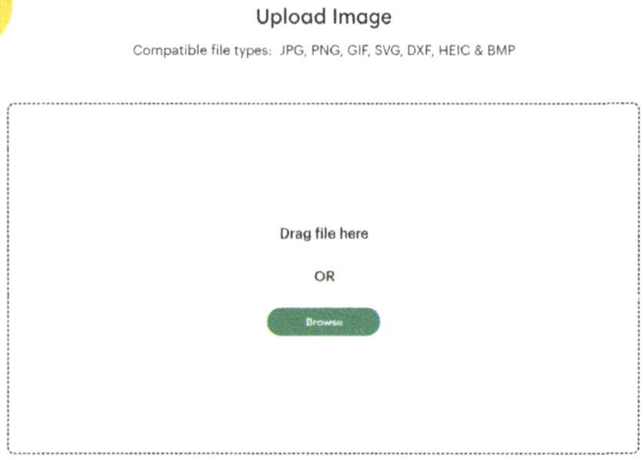

RE-EXPORT AND RE-UPLOAD: Fresh export fixes many issues, so if you created the file, re-export it from the original software and re-upload it to Design Space.

PNG UPLOADS AS A CUT FILE INSTEAD OF PRINT THEN CUT

Sometimes, a PNG file that you want to use for Design Space's Print Then Cut feature seems to upload as a cut file instead. Here's how to fix that problem.

1

CHECK THE FILE TYPE: Some files are mislabeled, so check the file type. Make sure the file ends in ".png."

2

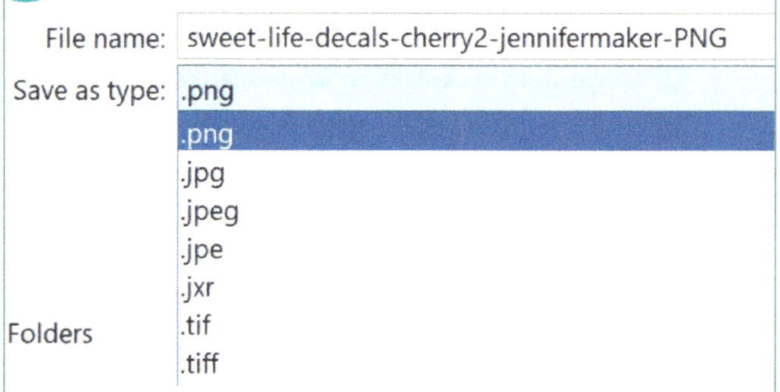

RESAVE IMAGE AS PNG: It's possible the image was saved as .jpg and renamed as .png, so resave it as a .png and re-upload it to Design Space.

3

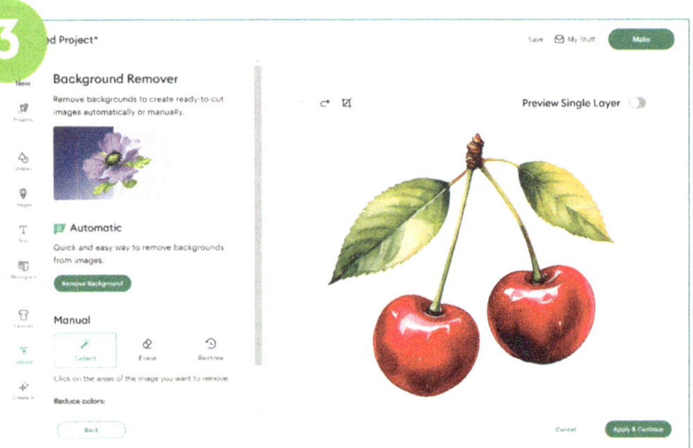

REMOVE BACKGROUND: Remove the background on the Background Remover screen. Even if the background looks transparent, it may actually be white.

4

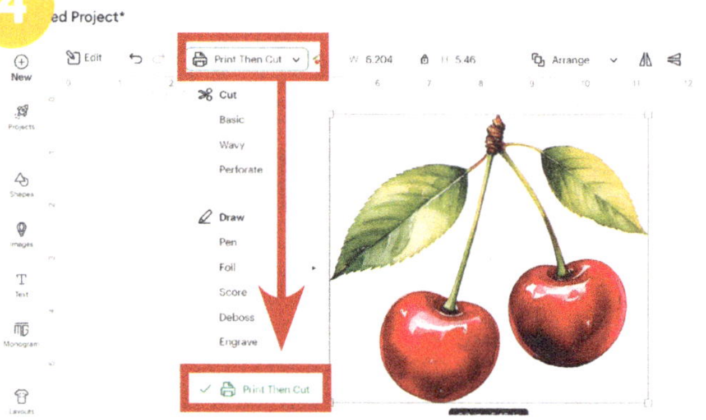

CHECK THE OPERATION: Make sure that the Operation is set to "Print Then Cut" on the Canvas by clicking on the design, then clicking the Operation drop-down menu in the top toolbar and selecting "Print Then Cut."

SOME LAYERS ARE MISSING OR MERGED

Are you missing layers of your design, or is it all one layer when it's supposed to be made up of multiple layers? There are a few reasons behind this, so try the options below to solve this problem.

1

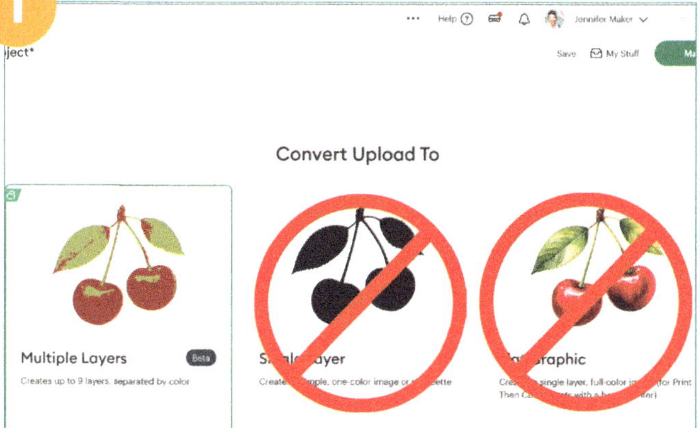

CHECK UPLOAD SETTINGS: "Flat Graphic" and "Single-layer" modes don't allow for multiple layers.

2

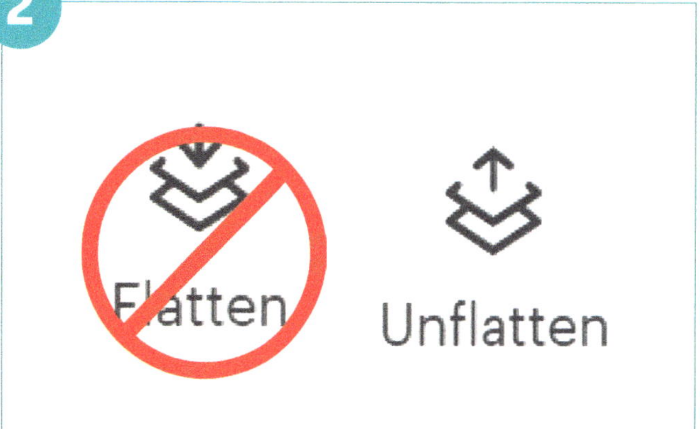

AVOID USING FLATTEN: Check to make sure that the layers haven't been "Flattened" together. If they have, select them and click "Unflatten."

3

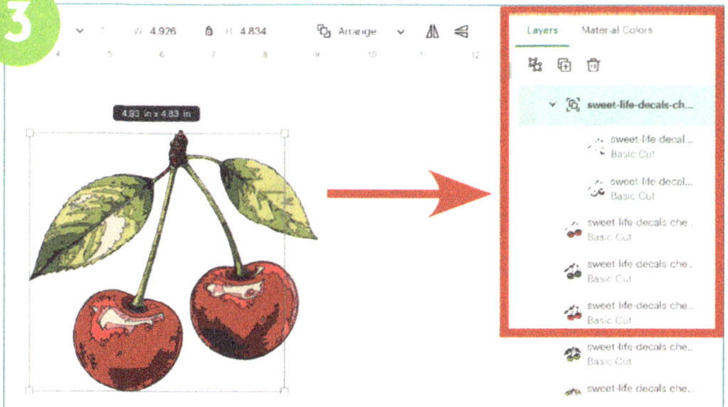

CHECK THE LAYERS PANEL: Hidden layers may exist, but may be nested within other layers inside the Layers Panel.

4

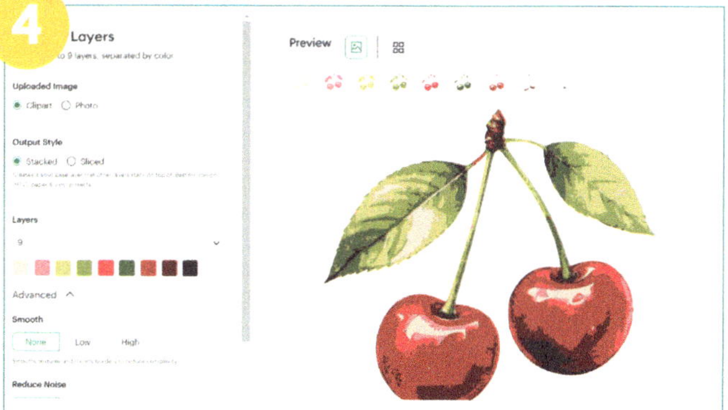

RE-UPLOAD WITH MULTIPLE LAYERS OPTION: SVG files are best for layered designs. You can separate a file into up to nine layers using the "Multiple Layers" option. NOTE: This is currently only available for Cricut Access Members.

"UPLOAD FAILED" ERRORS

Sometimes Cricut Design Space doesn't work right and your image or project fails to upload to the program. Here are a few reasons why that happens and solutions for each.

1

CHECK INTERNET CONNECTION: Uploads require stable internet. Don't switch connections mid-upload.

2

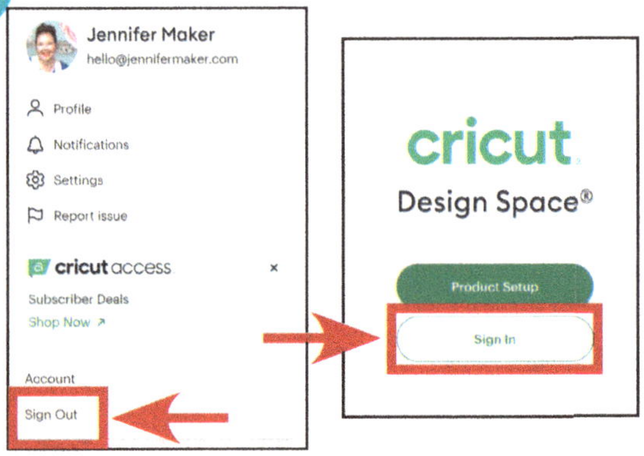

LOG OUT AND BACK IN: If Design Space has been open for a long time, the session can partially expire and block uploads.

3

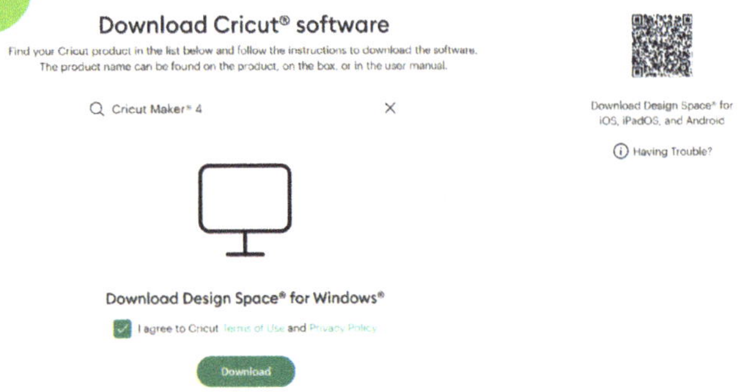

REINSTALL DESIGN SPACE: Sometimes a file needed for Design Space to properly operate can accidentally get deleted. Uninstall it from your device, then go to design.cricut.com to reinstall Design Space.

4

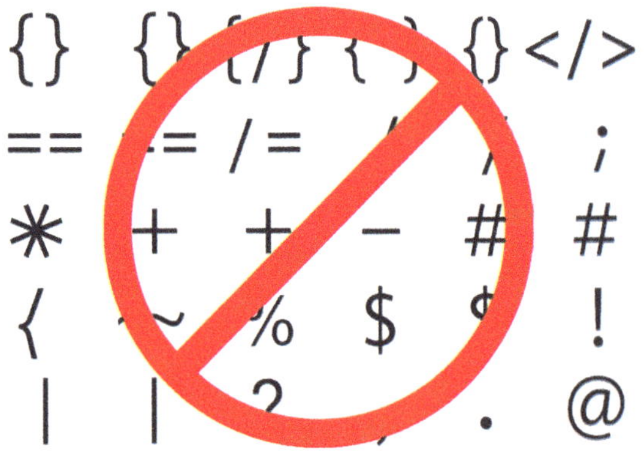

RENAME YOUR FILE: Avoid special characters, which are characters other than letters and numbers. Special characters can cause errors, compatibility issues, and misinterpreted commands.

PROJECTS ARE NOT SAVING

Is your project not saving, even though you've clicked "Save" or "Save As?" Are you unable to find the project you know you just saved? Try these tips to successfully save your projects.

1

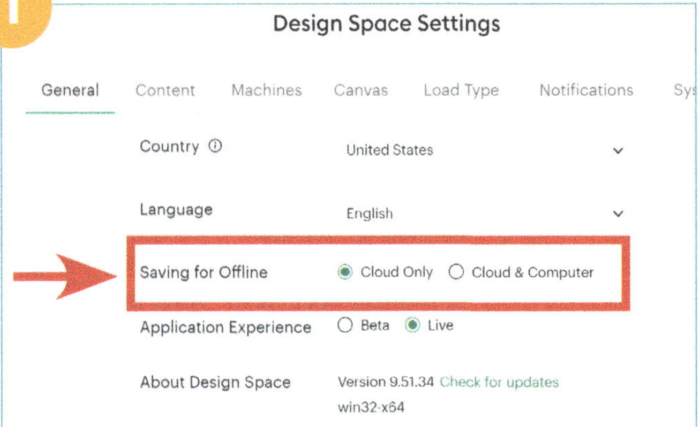

CHECK SAVE LOCATION: Are you saving to your device or the cloud? Click your name, then "Settings" to check where you're saving. If you saved to your device, are you using the same one you used to create the design?

2

CONFIRM YOU ARE ONLINE: Cloud saves require an internet connection that is strong and stable.

3

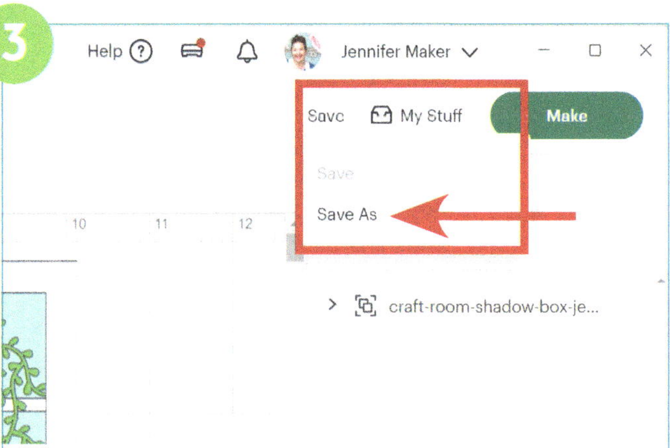

RENAME AND SAVE AGAIN: Try renaming your design and save using the "Save As" function instead of the "Save" function. This forces a new save instance.

4

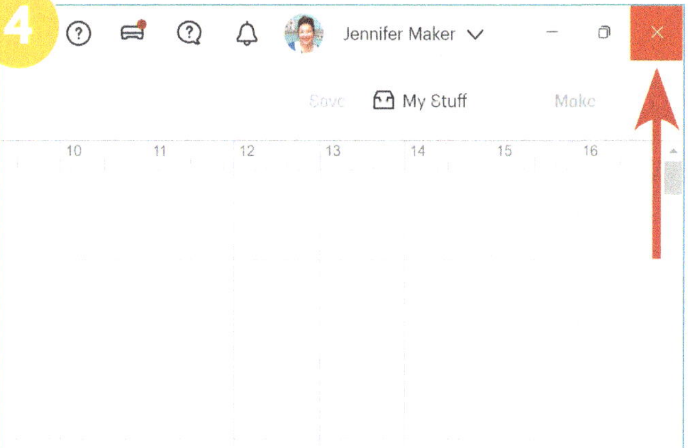

RESTART DESIGN SPACE: Close out of Design Space entirely, then start it up again. This fixes stuck save loops. Just be aware that you may lose some of your design progress.

PROJECTS ARE MISSING

Uh oh, what if you can't find a project that you know you saved? Here are some tips to help you find your missing projects.

1

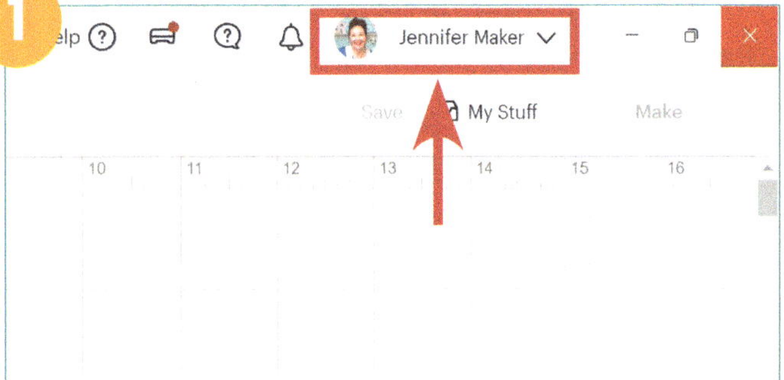

CHECK YOUR ACCOUNT NAME: Make sure you are logged into the right Cricut account by checking your account name and profile picture in the top right corner of the window.

2

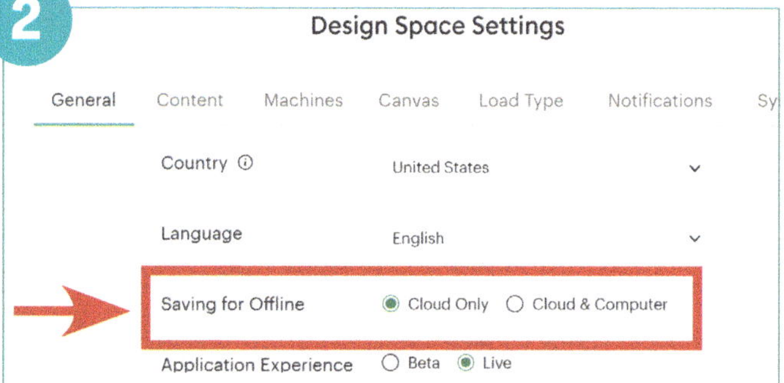

CONFIRM DEVICE VS CLOUD: Click your name, then "Settings" to check this. Device saves won't always appear if you're using a different device than usual.

3

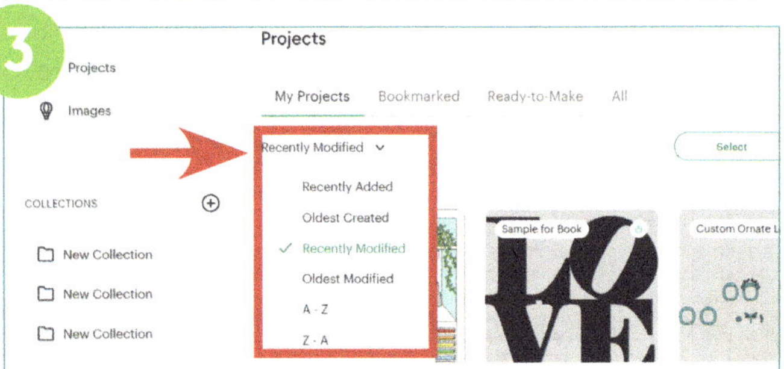

SORT BY DATE MODIFIED: Projects may be buried deep in your library, so while in the "Projects" menu, click "Recently Modified" and choose one of the other options.

4

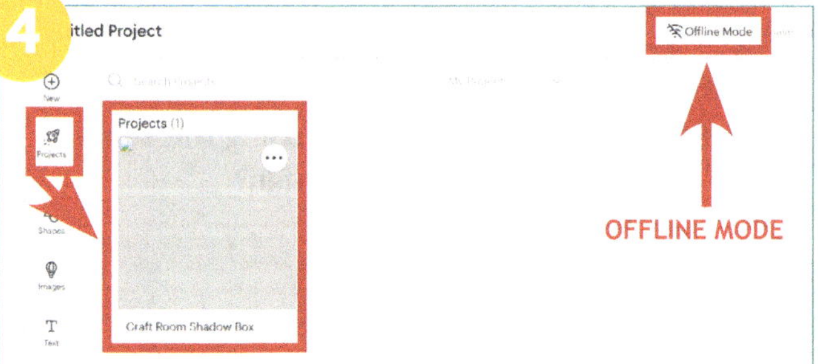

CHECK OFFLINE PROJECTS: Offline projects won't sync automatically. To find Offline projects, disconnect from the internet, then click on "Projects" to see your offline-saved projects.

5

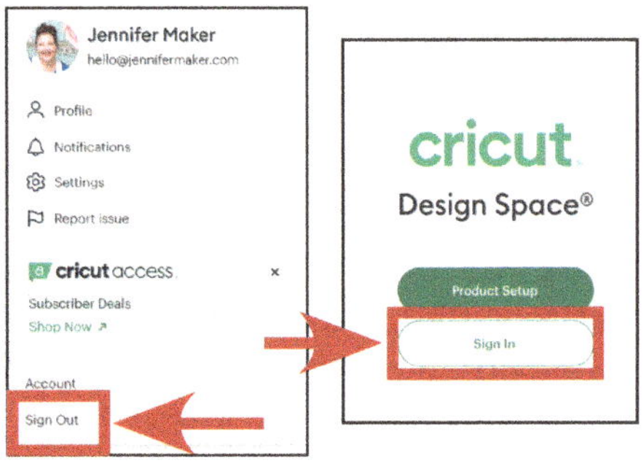

LOG OUT AND BACK IN: Log out of your Cricut account, then log back in. This triggers a project refresh.

6

WAIT FOR SYNC TO COMPLETE: Large libraries take time to load completely, so wait 30 seconds or so for everything to load.

OFFLINE VS CLOUD CONFUSION

Are you struggling to get projects that you saved offline to sync with your cloud-saved project library? Here's how to fix that problem.

1

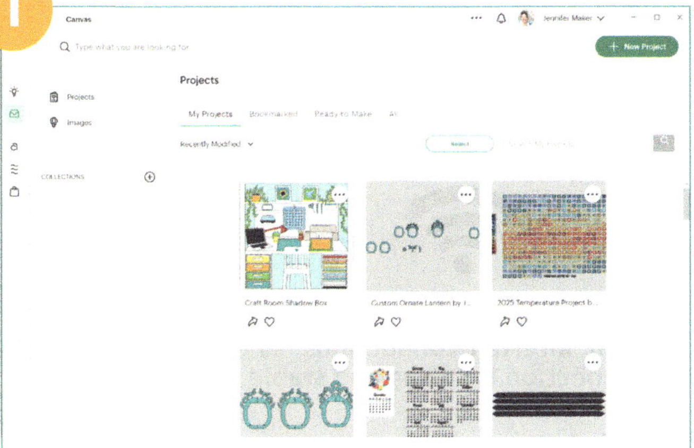

IDENTIFY WHERE THE PROJECT WAS SAVED: Projects saved offline are saved to your device. Projects saved to the cloud require an internet connection.

2

RECONNECT TO THE INTERNET: Disconnect from and reconnect to the internet to resync your projects saved to the cloud.

3

OPEN THE PROJECT ONLINE: Open Design Space, then connect to the internet. This automatically triggers cloud upload, so your offline projects will sync with the cloud.

4

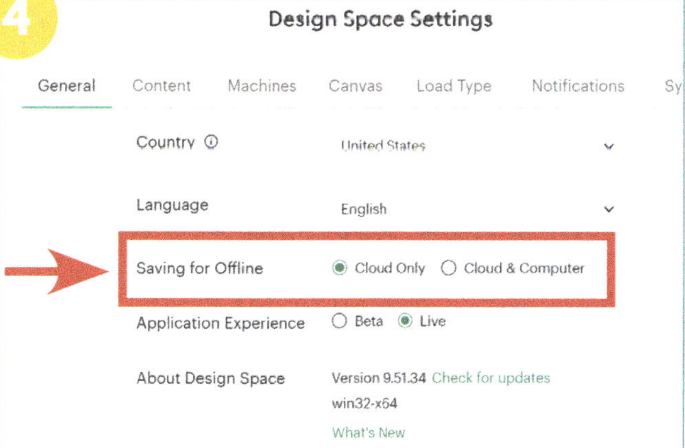

RESAVE TO CLOUD: In "Settings," switch your save method to "Cloud." Then save your project to the cloud so that it's available on any device you log in to.

ACCOUNT SYNC PROBLEMS

Sometimes, your account just isn't syncing and your projects aren't saving to your library where you can retrieve them. Here's how to problem-solve this issue.

1

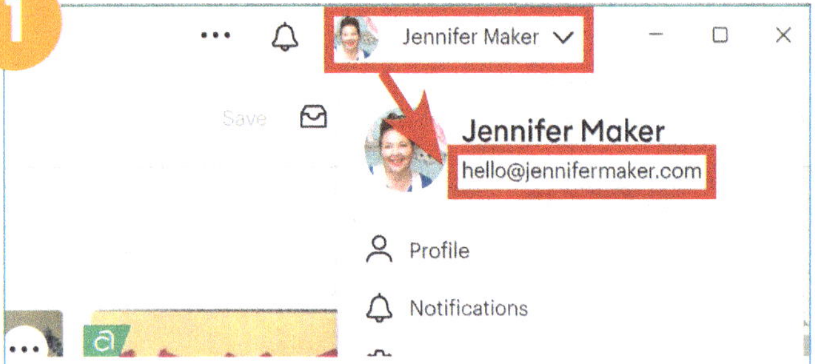

CONFIRM CORRECT LOGIN EMAIL: Cricut treats different emails as separate accounts. To check that you are using the right account, click your name and check the email in the pop-up window.

2

CHECK INTERNET STABILITY: Sync pauses on weak internet connections, so make sure your connection is strong and stable.

3

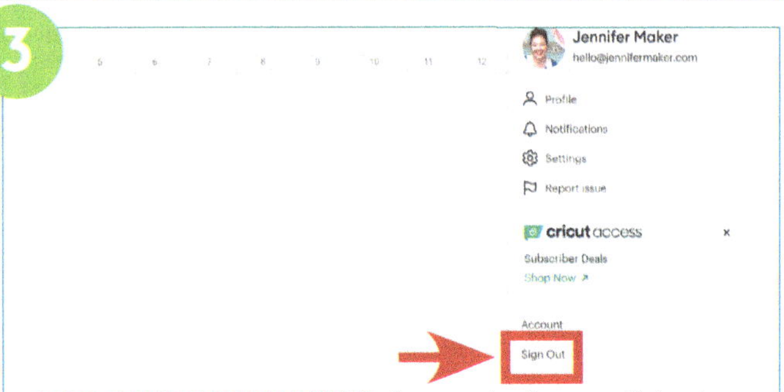

LOG OUT EVERYWHERE: Log out of your Cricut account on all devices you use it on. Click on your name, then click "Sign Out" in the pop-up window.This clears stuck sessions.

4

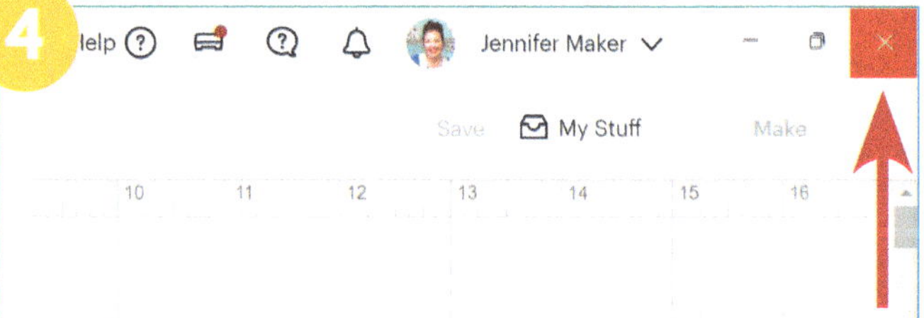

CLOSE OUT AND RESTART THE APP: This is required after logging out of your account, so close Design Space completely and then restart it. On a Mac, go to the Cricut Design Space menu in the upper left corner and choose Quit.

5

WAIT FOR FULL SYNC: Don't close the app early. Wait about 30 seconds for everything to finish syncing.

6

CONTACT CRICUT SUPPORT: If problems persist, try contacting Cricut Support at 1-877-727-4288 or help.cricut.com. Account-level issues require intervention.

CUTTING PROBLEMS

- Machine Not Turning On
- Machine Freezing Mid-Cut
- Carriage Slamming or Jerking
- Machine Not Recognizing Tools
- Wrong Clamp Being Used
- Tool Compatibility Issues
- Inconsistent Cut Depth
- Double or Misaligned Cuts
- Cricut Machine is Not Connecting
- Cricut is Stuck on the Prepare Screen
- Bluetooth vs. USB Issues
- Firmware Problems
- Design is the Wrong Size
- Design Shifted While Cutting
- Cut Doesn't Match the Preview
- Cricut is Cutting Slow
- Too Many Layers Slowing Down Your Cut
- Design Space is Running Slow
- Break Big Projects Into Smaller Parts
- Reduce Node Overload (When Possible)
- Mat Not Loading Straight
- Cricut Isn't Cutting All the Way Through
- Cricut is Overcutting
- Material is Dragging or Tearing
- Blade Depth vs. Pressure: What's the Difference?

MACHINE NOT TURNING ON

When your Cricut won't power up, it can feel scary, but most causes are simple and fixable. Let's walk through quick power checks to rule out cords, outlets, and startup hiccups.

1

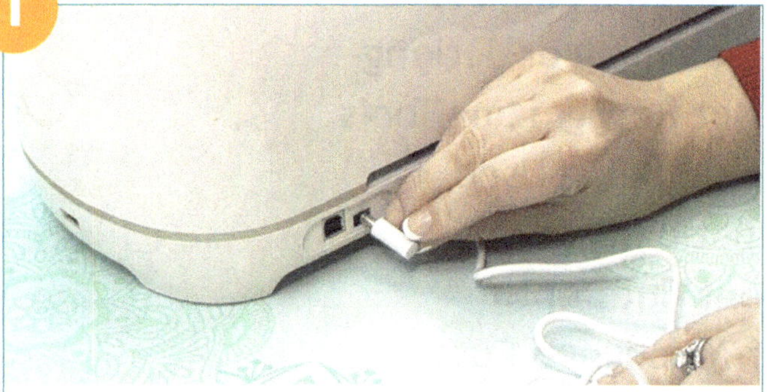

CHECK THE POWER CONNECTION AT BOTH ENDS OF THE CORD: Even if the cord looks plugged in, it may not be fully seated. Push the cord firmly into the back of the Cricut machine and the wall outlet so it does not wiggle. Be sure to use the correct power cord for your machine — they are not interchangeable.

2

PLUG DIRECTLY INTO A WALL OUTLET: Power strips and surge protectors can sometimes reduce voltage just enough to prevent the machine from powering on. For testing, always plug the Cricut directly into a wall outlet by itself or if it is already plugged directly in, change wall outlets.

3

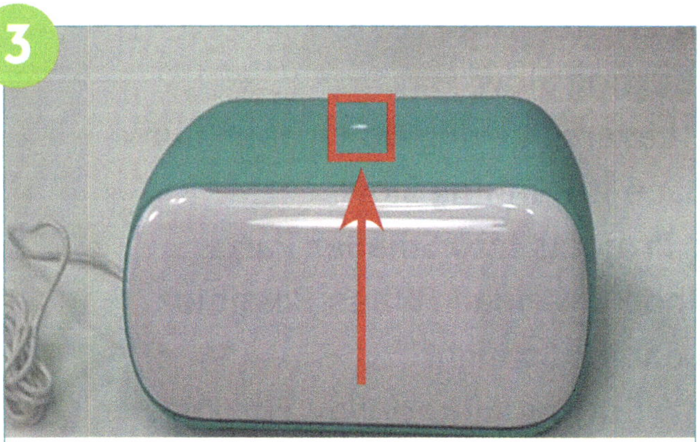

LOOK CLOSELY FOR ANY INDICATOR LIGHTS OR SOUNDS: A completely dark machine usually indicates a power issue, while blinking lights can point to firmware or startup problems.

4

PERFORM A FULL POWER CYCLE: Unplug the machine completely and leave it unplugged for at least 30 to 60 seconds. This clears residual power and allows the machine to restart fresh when plugged back in.

MACHINE FREEZING MID-CUT

A frozen cut is frustrating, especially when you've already loaded your material. These steps help you safely stop, reset, and restart without ruining alignment or damage.

1

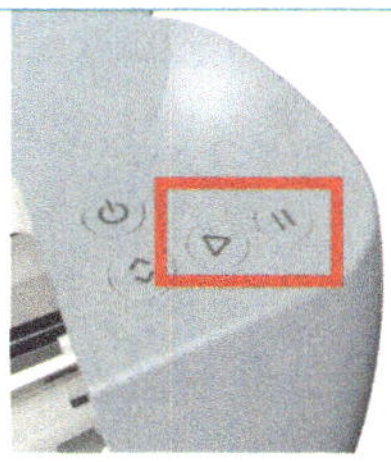

PAUSE AND AVOID TOUCHING THE MAT IMMEDIATELY: Press the Start/Pause button on your machine. Give the software a moment to respond before taking action. Pulling the mat or forcing movement can permanently misalign the cut.

2

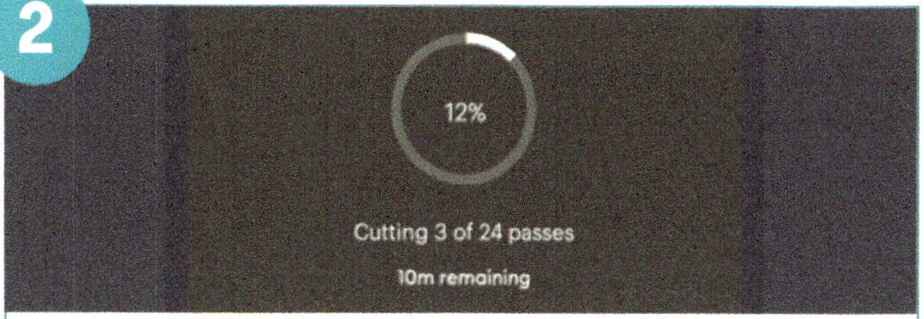

CHECK DESIGN SPACE FOR RESPONSIVENESS: If the progress bar is frozen or spinning, the issue is usually communication-related. The machine often stops because Design Space stopped sending instructions. If you are using a mobile device, be sure to keep it close to your Cricut while cutting to avoid communication issues.

3

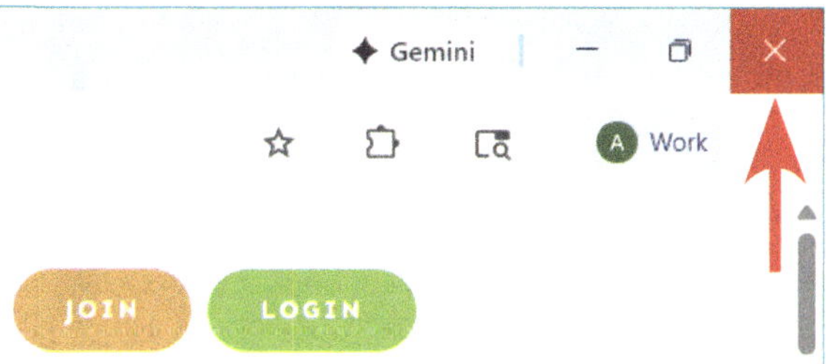

CLOSE UNNECESSARY PROGRAMS OR BROWSER TABS: Large or detailed designs require significant memory to process. Background programs can overload your device and cause Design Space to freeze.

4

CANCEL THE CUT FROM DESIGN SPACE IF POSSIBLE: Canceling from the software keeps the machine and canvas aligned. Avoid powering off unless the software is completely unresponsive.

5

POWER OFF THE MACHINE SAFELY: Turn the machine off using the power button or by unplugging your machine and wait 60 seconds before plugging it back in and turning it back on. This allows internal components to reset properly.

6

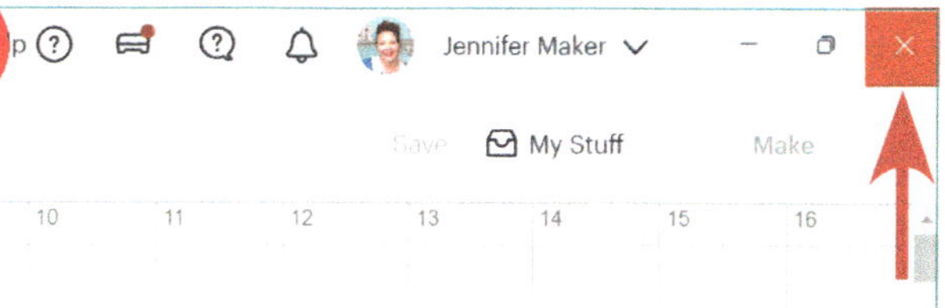

RESTART DESIGN SPACE COMPLETELY: Close completely out of design space by clicking the X in the upper right corner on a Windows computer or on a Mac go to the Cricut Design Space menu in the upper left corner and clicking Quit.

CARRIAGE SLAMMING OR JERKING

Loud jerks or sudden slamming are a sign something isn't right, and continuing can cause damage. Here's how to stop the issue immediately and safely get your machine moving.

1

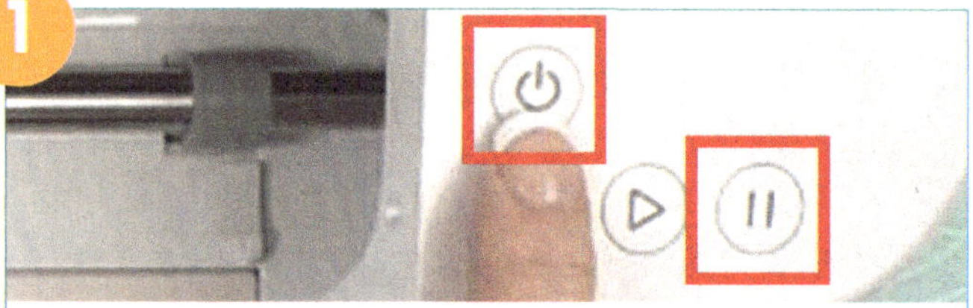

STOP THE CUT IMMEDIATELY: Press pause or turn off the machine as soon as you notice abnormal movement. Continued operation can damage internal motors. Joy users need to unplug the cord from the back of the machine to power it off.

2

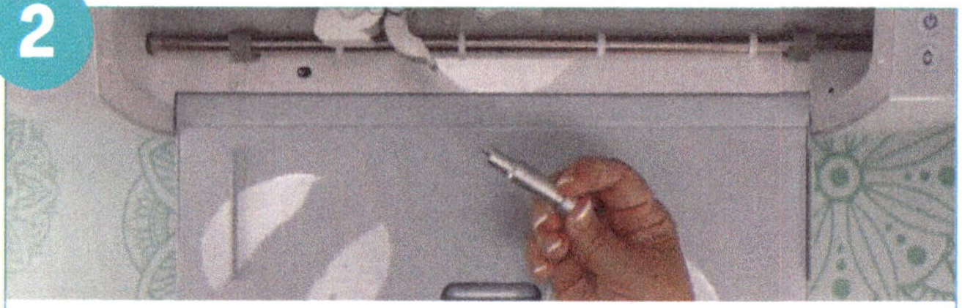

CHECK TOOL & MACHINE DISTANCE FROM WALL: A blade that is slightly loose or improperly seated can cause erratic movement. Take it out completely and check for debris or damage by pushing the plunger to expose the blade. Be sure that your machine is away from the wall to allow the mat to move through freely.

3

CHECK THE MAT AND MATERIAL: Tape edges, curled material, or thick seams can block carriage movement. Remove anything that could interfere with smooth travel.

4

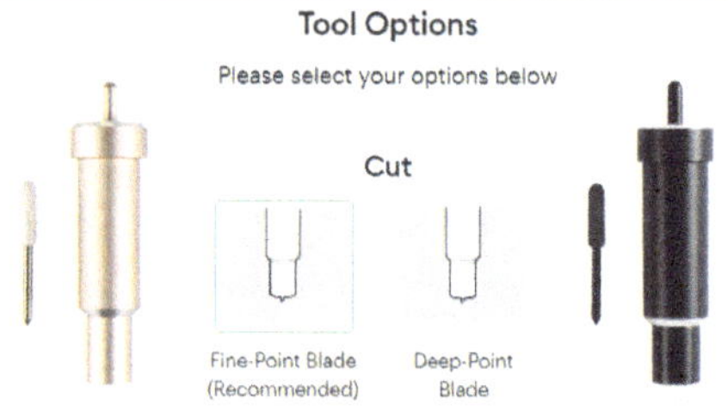

CONFIRM THE CORRECT TOOL IS INSTALLED: Using the wrong blade increases resistance and stresses the carriage. Always match the tool to the material requirements. The Scoring tool and Rotary tool are often confused so be sure to double-check that the right tool in installed.

5

RESEAT THE TOOL CAREFULLY AND FIRMLY: The tool should drop fully into the clamp and sit straight, not angled or raised. Close the clamp securely without forcing it.

6

RUN A SMALL TEST CUT BEFORE CONTINUING: Never resume a full project immediately after a carriage issue. A test cut confirms the problem is resolved safely.

MACHINE NOT RECOGNIZING TOOLS

If Design Space keeps asking for a tool you've already installed, don't panic. This will help you reseat, refresh, and verify tool detection step by step.

1

REMOVE AND REINSERT THE TOOL SLOWLY: Lift the clamp fully before inserting the tool. This ensures the tool seats properly and makes contact with the sensor.

2

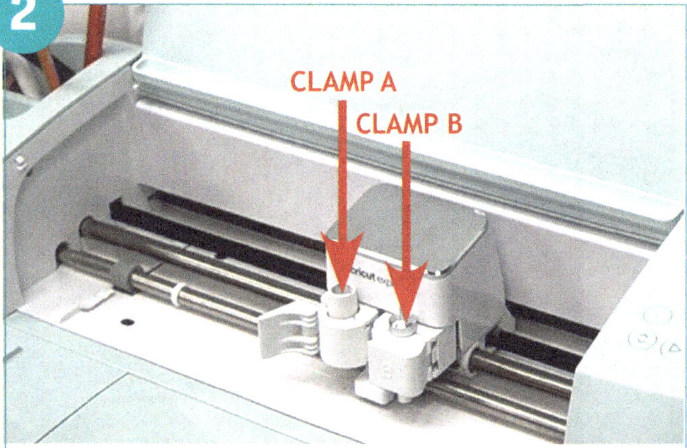

VERIFY THE TOOL IS IN THE CORRECT CLAMP: Clamp A is for accessories like a scoring stylus and pens, while Clamp B is for cutting blades. Using the wrong clamp prevents detection.

3

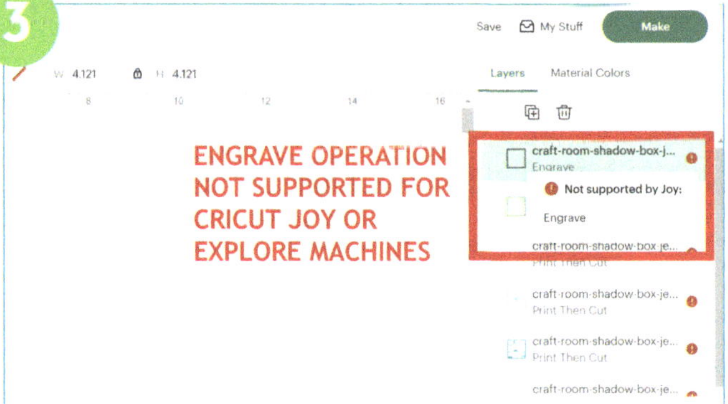

CONFIRM THE TOOL IS COMPATIBLE WITH YOUR MACHINE: Not all Cricut machines support all tools. If an option is missing, it means the tool isn't supported. You will see a warning in the Layers Panel if you switch to an incompatible machine.

4

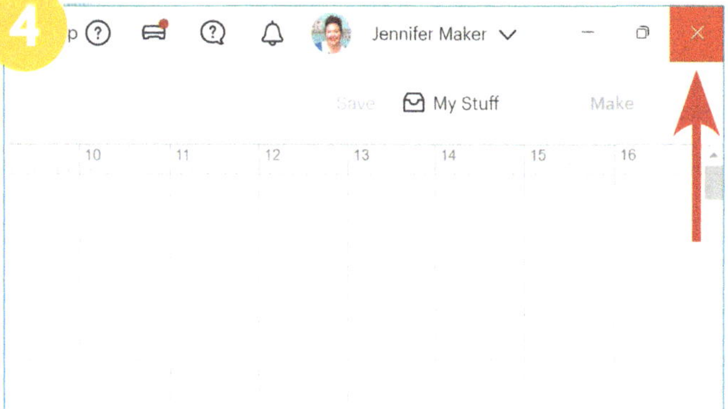

RESTART DESIGN SPACE TO REFRESH DETECTION: Closing and reopening Design Space forces the software to recheck installed tools. This often resolves recognition issues immediately. So save, close out of Design Space, and restart it.

NOTE: The scoring wheel and rotary tool look similar, so they're easy to mix up on a Maker. Double-check before starting your cut.

WRONG CLAMP BEING USED

On Explore, Maker, and Venture machines, clamp mix-ups are one of the most common Cricut mistakes. This will make it easy to remember which clamp does what and how to recover if they get switched.

1

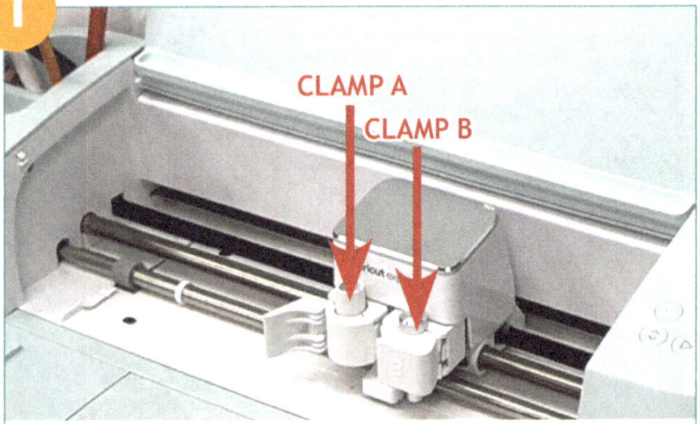

UNDERSTAND THE BASIC CLAMP RULE: Clamp A always holds accessories, and Clamp B always holds cutting blades. Mixing them up can cause errors or damage.

2

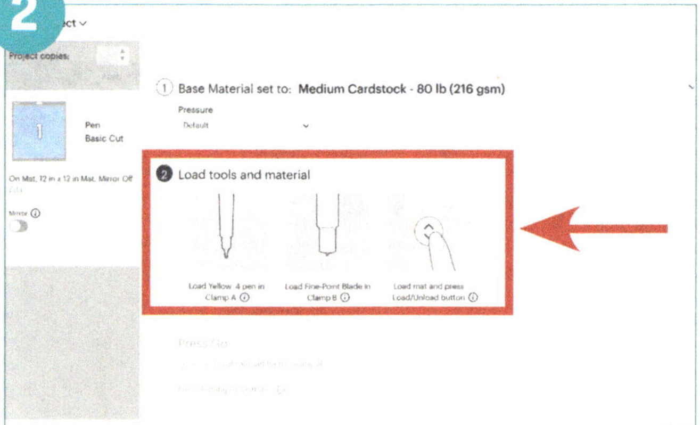

FOLLOW THE ON-SCREEN PROMPT EXACTLY: Design Space will tell you which clamp to use at each step. Start with the tools shown on the Prepare screen, then switch when prompted. Trust the prompt rather than guessing.

3

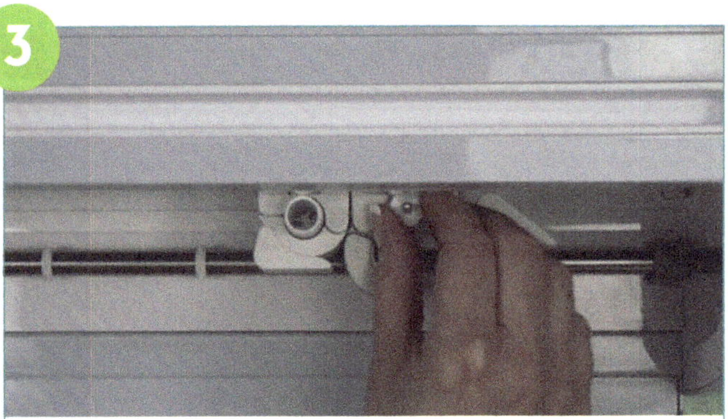

NEVER SWITCH CLAMPS MID-PROMPT: Changing clamps without canceling the cut can confuse the machine. Only insert/remove tools from the clamps when prompted. Always stop and reset if a mistake is made.

4

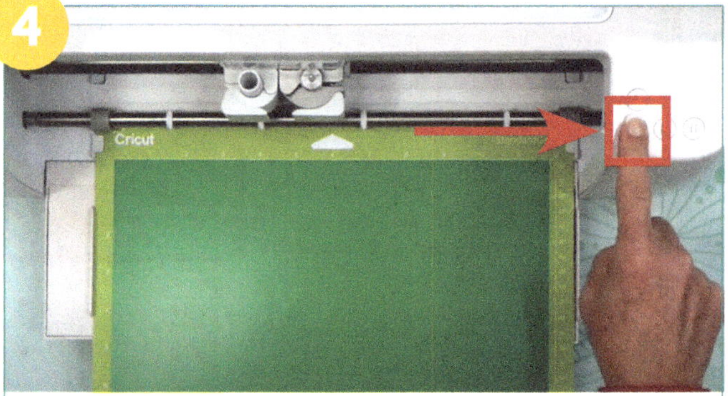

UNLOAD AND RELOAD THE MAT AFTER CORRECTING: This resets the tool sequence and prevents misalignment. It ensures the machine starts fresh, so press the Load/Unload button to unload the mat, then reinsert and load the mat. again.

TOOL COMPATIBILITY ISSUES

Not every Cricut tool works with every machine or material. Here's how to confirm compatibility so you don't waste time, materials, or blades.

1

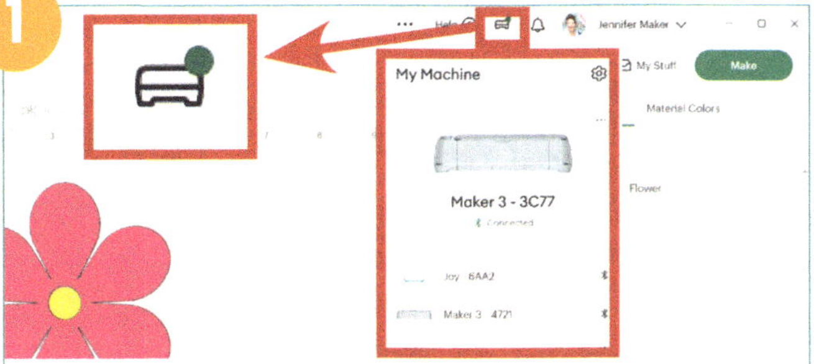

CONFIRM WHICH CRICUT MACHINE YOU ARE USING: Different machines support different tools. Click the machine icon at the top of the Design Space window and see which machine is connected.

2

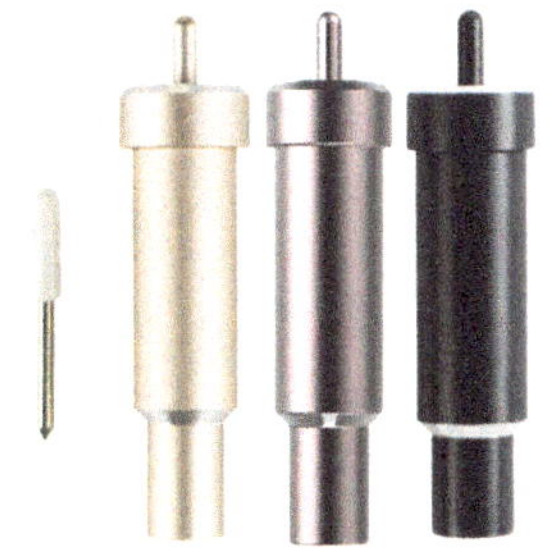

CHECK THE TOOL HOUSING COLOR AND TYPE CAREFULLY: Some housings look similar but are designed for different blades. Using the wrong housing affects cut behavior.

3

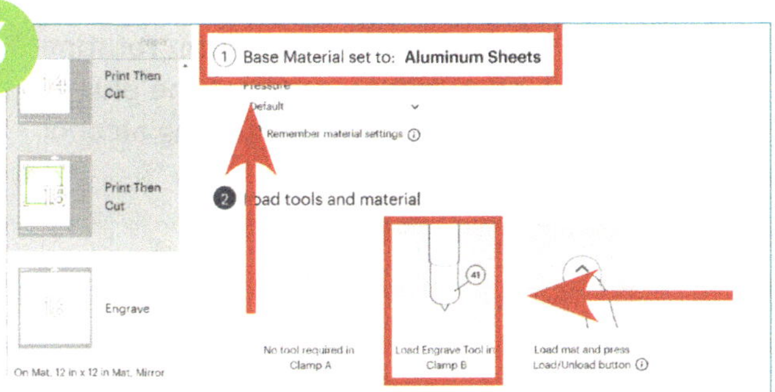

VERIFY MATERIAL REQUIREMENTS FOR THE TOOL: The Engrave and Knife Blades and specialty tools only work on approved materials. Unsupported materials can cause failures.

4

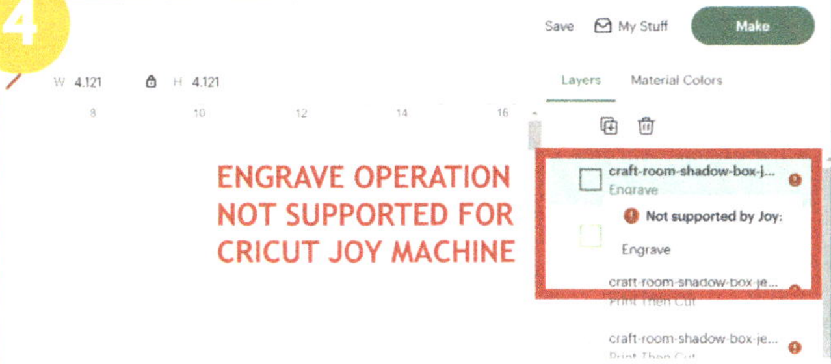

LOOK FOR WARNING SIGNS IN THE LAYERS PANEL: Warning signs that indicate incompatibility are due to the machine you are using, not a software error. Design Space is preventing misuse.

5

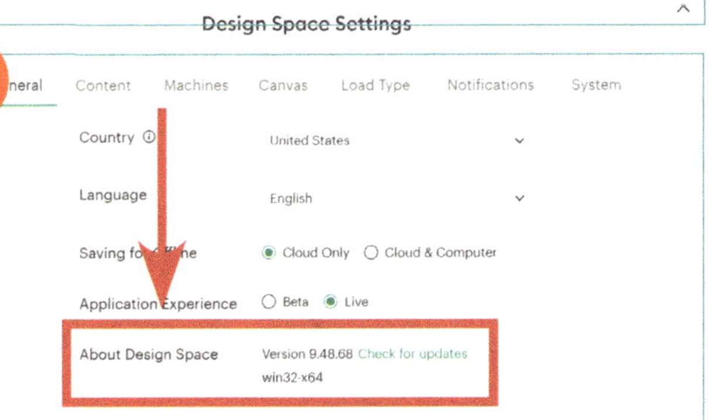

UPDATE FIRMWARE: New tools often require firmware updates to function. Click on your name, then "Settings," then "Check for Updates."

6

TEST WITH A BASIC MATERIAL AND BLADE: Testing with cardstock or vinyl isolates whether the issue is tool-related or system-related.

INCONSISTENT CUT DEPTH

When some areas cut perfectly and others barely cut at all, something is interfering with pressure or stability. These checks help you restore even, clean cuts across your entire project.

1

CLEAN YOUR MAT: If parts of the mat have lost stickiness, the material may lift slightly during cutting. This causes some areas to cut fully while others barely cut at all. Clean your mat to restore even stickiness.

2

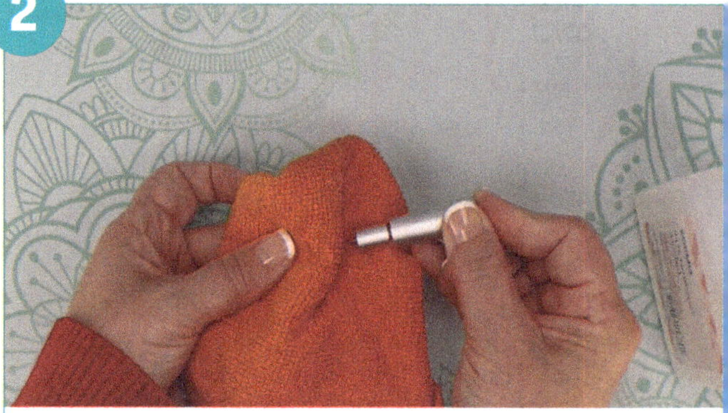

INSPECT THE BLADE FOR DEBRIS OR BUILDUP: Tiny fibers, dust, and glitter can get trapped around the blade and prevent it from rotating freely. Clean off debris by pressing the plunger to expose the blade and using rubbing alcohol and a thick microfiber cloth.

3

MAKE SURE THE MATERIAL IS COMPLETELY FLAT ON THE MAT: Warped or curled materials create uneven pressure under the blade. Use a brayer to press the material firmly from the center outward.

4

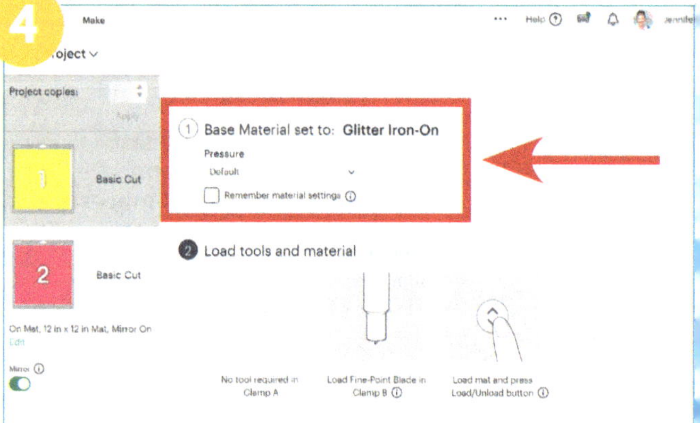

VERIFY THE CORRECT MATERIAL SETTING IS SELECTED: An incorrect material setting may apply inconsistent pressure. Match the setting to the material's behavior, not just its name.

DOUBLE OR MISALIGNED CUTS

If your design is cutting twice or no longer lining up, it's usually a setup issue, not your machine. Here's how to spot hidden layers and prevent shifting.

1

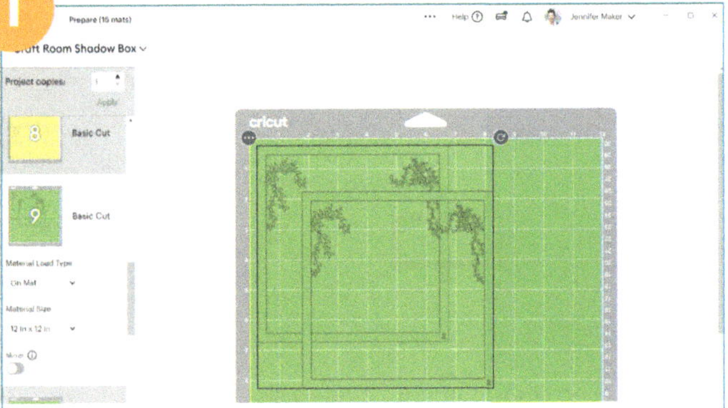

CHECK FOR DUPLICATE OR HIDDEN LAYERS: Accidental duplicates that are Attached together are easy to miss and will cause the design to cut twice. Always inspect the Layers panel and Mat Previews before cutting.

2

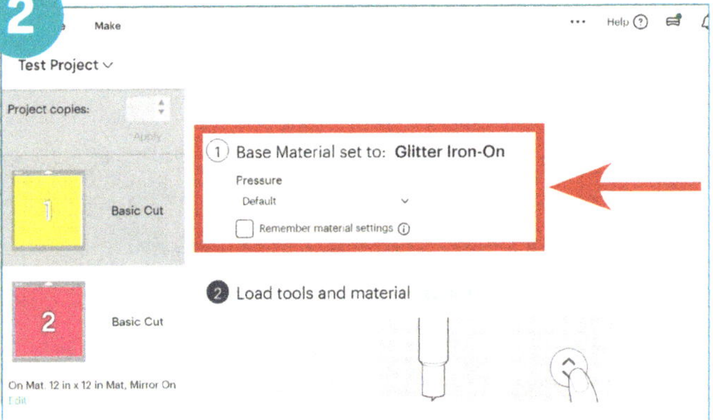

AVOID USING EXCESSIVE PRESSURE SETTINGS: Too much pressure can cause the blade to drag or pull the material. Dragging leads to shifting and inaccurate cuts. So always start with "Default" Pressure before moving to "More" Pressure.

3

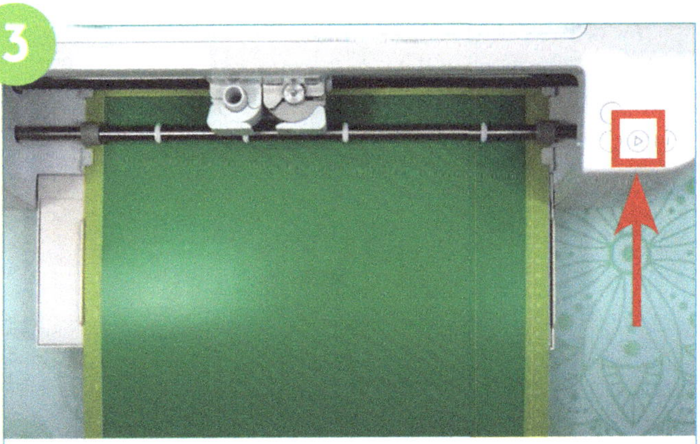

DON'T UNLOAD THE MAT BETWEEN MULTIPLE CUTS: If you want your mat to cut a second time, immediately press the Go button on your Cricut machine or in Design Space if using a Joy or Joy Xtra. Don't remove and reinsert the mat.

4

RELOAD THE MAT CAREFULLY AND STRAIGHT: If the mat is loaded at a slight angle, the cut path may not align correctly. Always start over completely by unloading the mat, using fresh material, and reloading if alignment looks off.

CRICUT MACHINE IS NOT CONNECTING

If your Cricut isn't showing up in Design Space or won't connect, don't worry -- this is a very common issue. Most connection problems can be fixed in just a few quick steps, and it rarely means something is wrong with your machine.

1

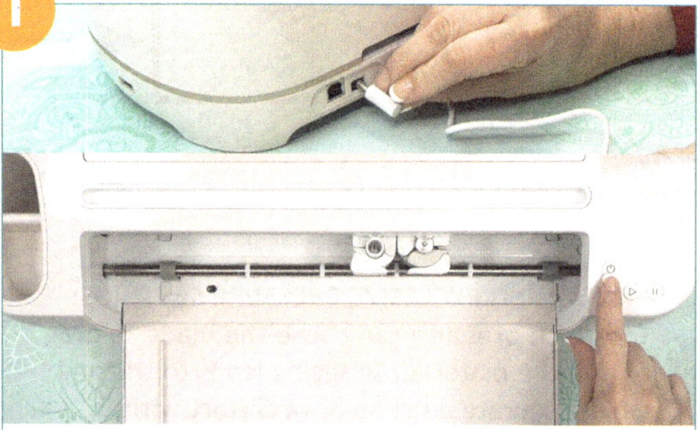

CHECK POWER AND BASICS: Make sure your Cricut is turned on and plugged in. Look for the power light and confirm the machine is awake -- not sleeping.

2

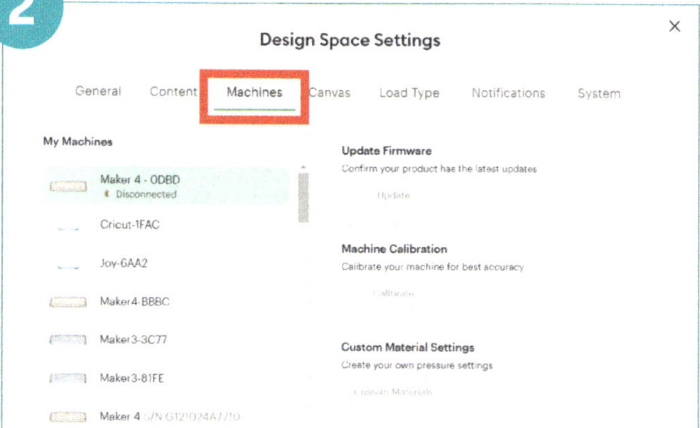

CONFIRM THE MACHINE IN DESIGN SPACE: Open Design Space, click on your name in the upper-right, and click "Settings." Click "Machines" and check under "My Machines". If your Cricut isn't listed, it isn't connected yet.

3

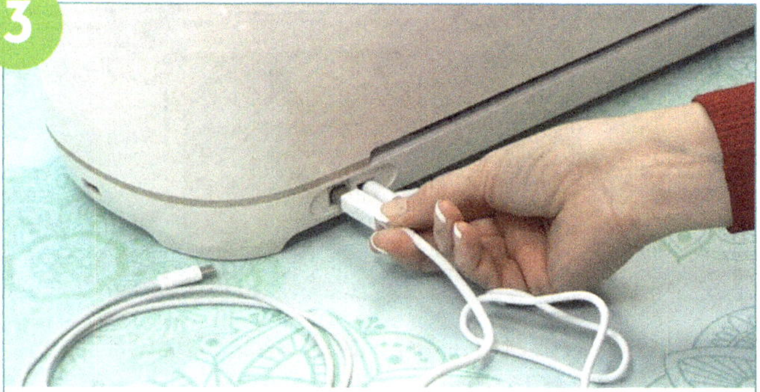

RECONNECT THE MACHINE: If using Bluetooth, remove the Cricut from your device's Bluetooth list and pair it again. For Explore, Maker, and Venture machines, try connecting with a USB cable to rule out wireless issues.

4

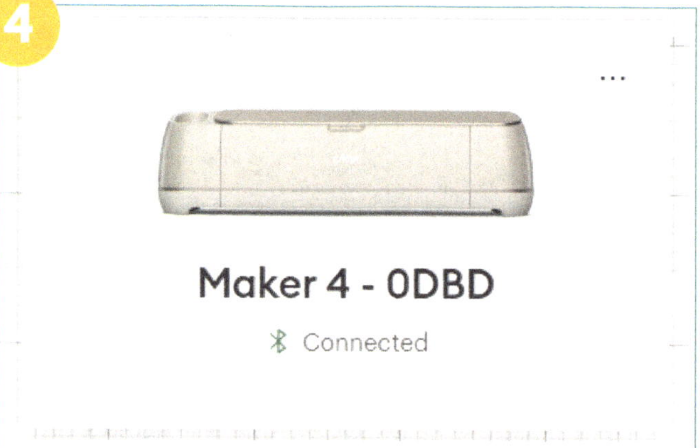

RESTART AND TRY AGAIN: Close Design Space completely, restart your computer or tablet, then reopen Design Space and reconnect the machine.

CRICUT IS STUCK ON THE PREPARE SCREEN

Getting stuck on the Prepare screen can be frustrating, especially when you're ready to cut. This usually means Design Space needs a quick reset. Follow these steps to get your project moving again.

1

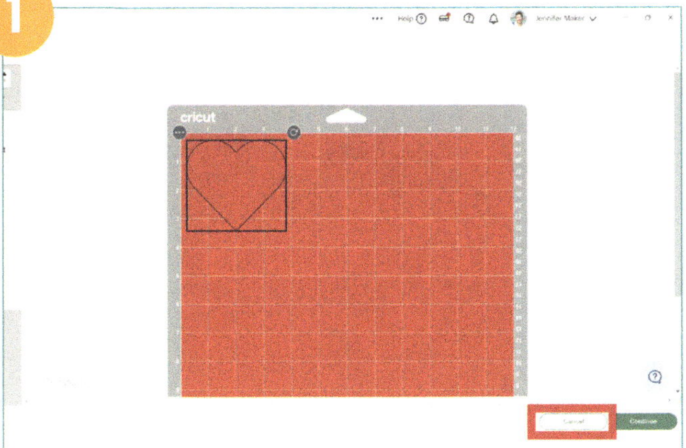

CANCEL THE CUT: Click "Cancel" and stop the process -- don't wait it out. If it's stuck, it usually won't fix itself.

2

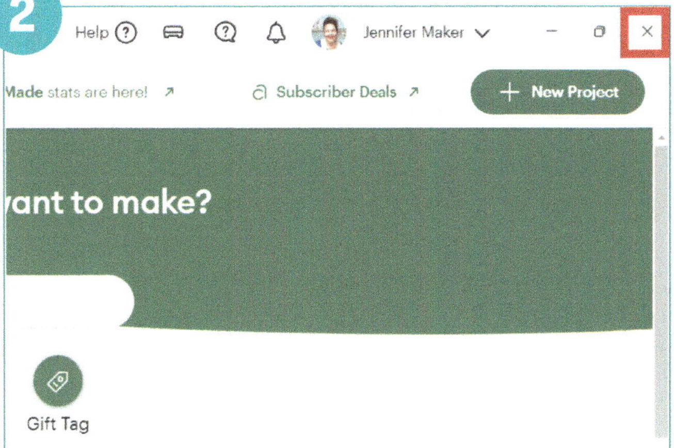

CLOSE DESIGN SPACE: Fully close Design Space (not just the browser tab or app window). This clears temporary glitches.

3

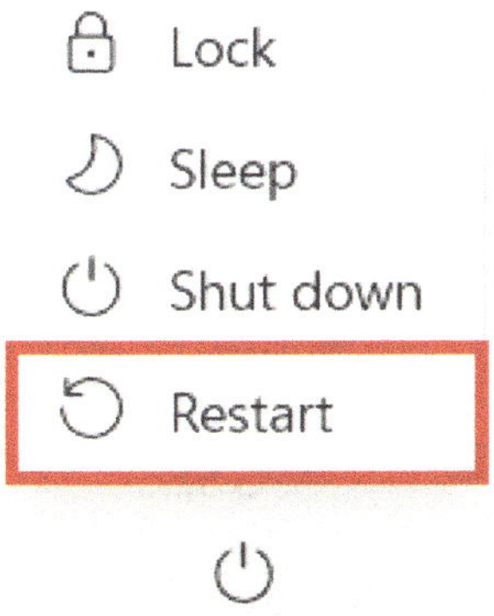

RESTART YOUR DEVICE: Restart your computer, tablet, or phone to free up memory and reset background processes.

4

REOPEN AND TRY AGAIN: Open Design Space, reload your project, and click "Make" again. In many cases, this fixes the issue immediately.

BLUETOOTH VS USB ISSUES

Bluetooth is convenient, but it isn't always the most reliable option. If your cuts freeze, fail, or disconnect, switching how your Cricut connects can make all the difference.

1

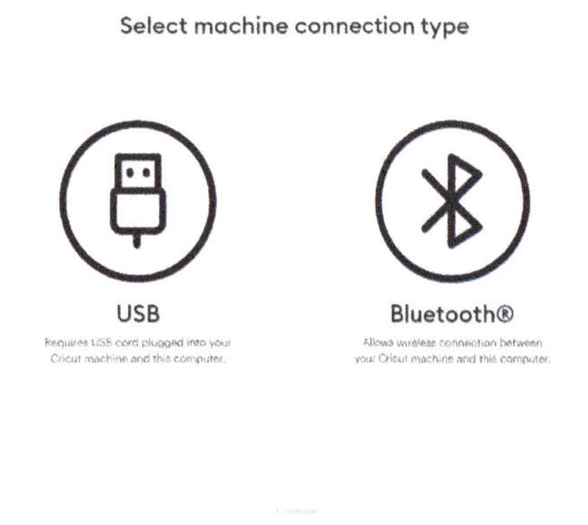

KNOW THE DIFFERENCE: Bluetooth is convenient, but USB is more stable. If things feel glitchy, the connection may be the problem.

2

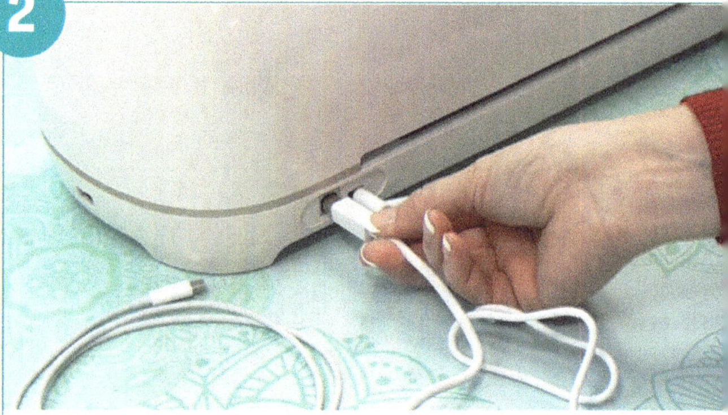

SWITCH TO USB: Plug your Cricut directly into your computer with a USB cable (if your machine has one, Joy Xtra does not) and try the cut again.

3

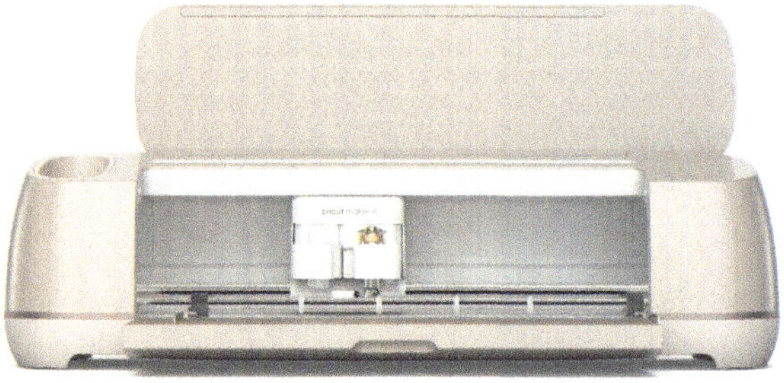

REDUCE INTERFERENCE: If you prefer Bluetooth, move closer to the machine and turn off other nearby Bluetooth devices that could interfere.

4

CHOOSE RELIABILITY FOR BIG PROJECTS: For long or important cuts, use USB whenever possible – it's my go-to for troubleshooting and stress-free cutting.

FIRMWARE PROBLEMS

Firmware issues can cause all kinds of strange behavior, but they're usually easy to fix. These steps will help you safely update your machine and get everything running smoothly again.

1

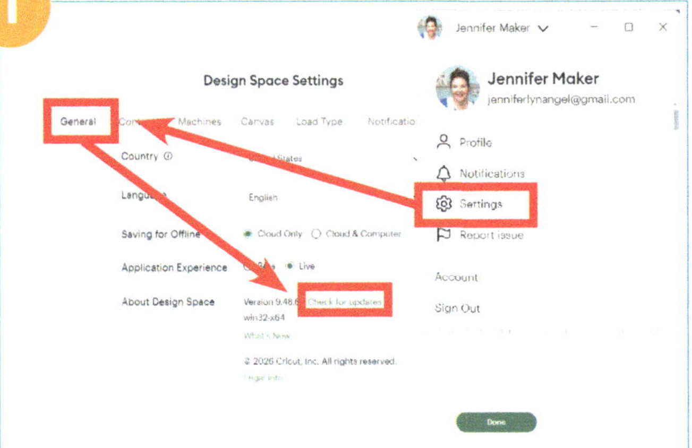

OPEN MACHINE SETTINGS: In Design Space, click on your name and "Settings." Under "General" click "Check for Updates" to check the firmware status.

2

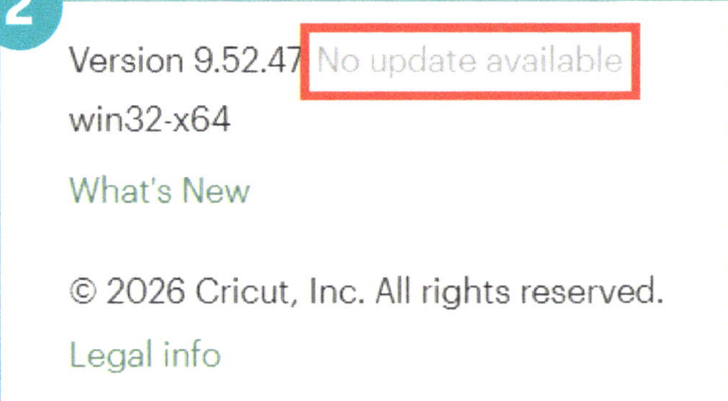

RUN FIRMWARE UPDATE: If an update is available, start it and follow the prompts carefully.

3

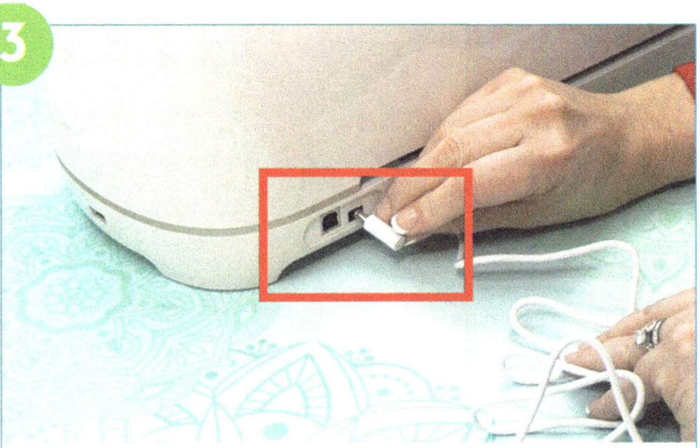

DON'T INTERRUPT THE UPDATE: Do not unplug the machine or close Design Space while firmware is updating. Let it finish completely.

4

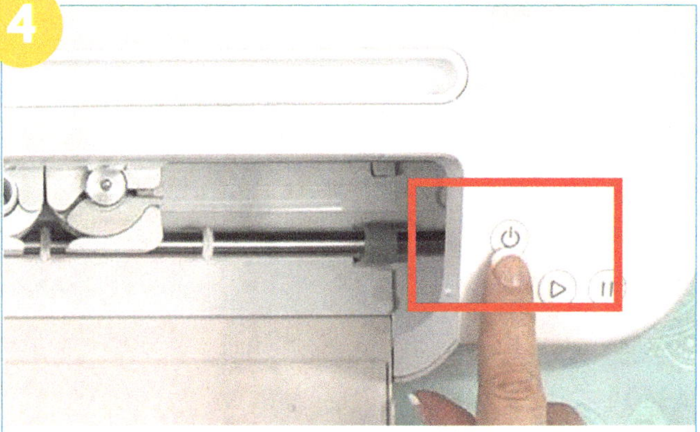

RESTART AFTER UPDATING: Once the update is complete, restart your Cricut and your device before starting a new project.

DESIGN IS THE WRONG SIZE

If your cut looks bigger or smaller than you expected, don't worry. This is usually a quick sizing check on the Canvas. These steps will help you confirm the design size before you cut so your project turns out exactly right.

1

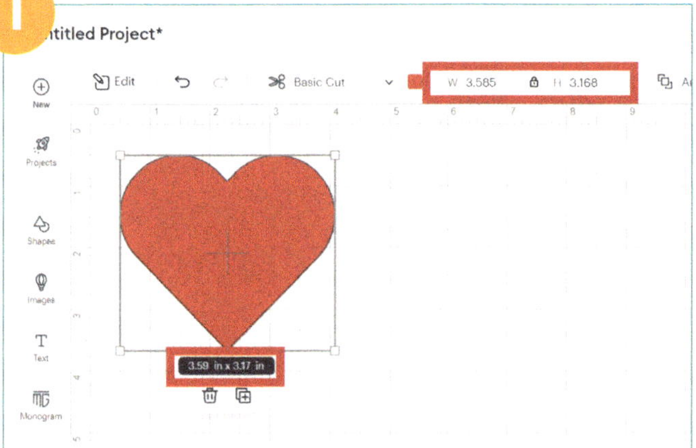

CHECK THE SIZE ON THE CANVAS: Click on your design and look at the width and height either in the top toolbar or under the design. This is the actual size your Cricut will cut, not just how it looks on your screen.

2

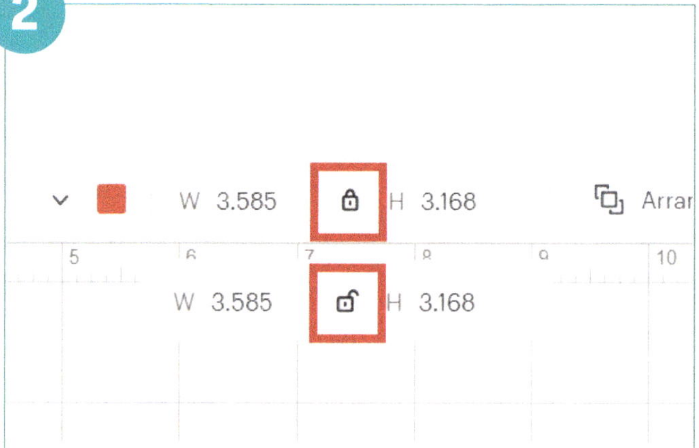

USE THE LOCK ICON CORRECTLY: If you want your design to stay proportional, make sure the lock icon is turned on (closed) before resizing. If the lock is off (open), your design can stretch or shrink unevenly.

3

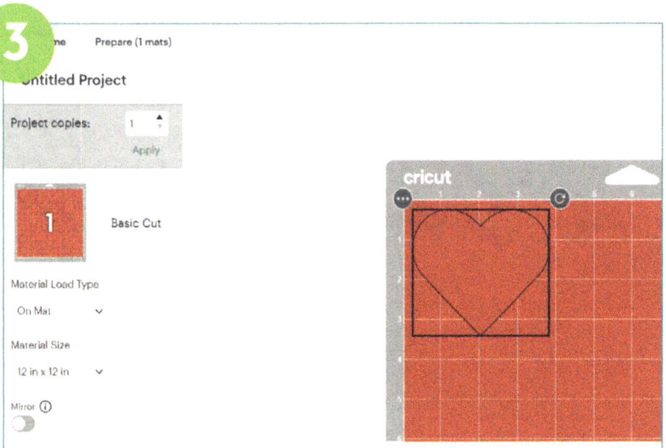

CONFIRM THE SIZE IN THE MAT PREVIEW: Click "Make" and double-check the size in the mat preview. This shows exactly how large your design will be when it cuts.

4

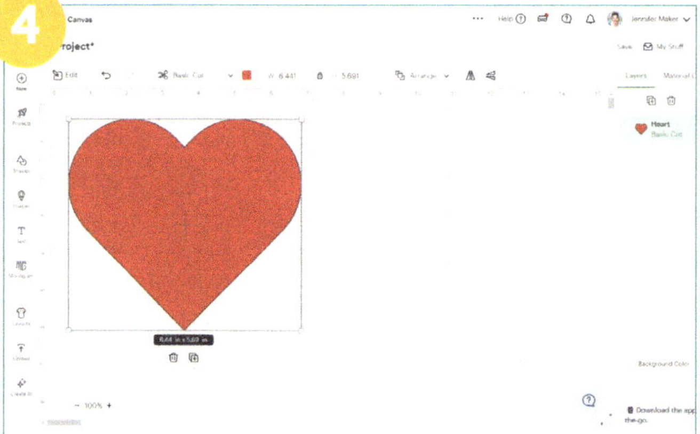

RESIZE BEFORE CUTTING: If the size isn't right, go back to the Canvas, adjust it, and click "Make" again. Taking a moment here can save a lot of material.

DESIGN SHIFTED WHILE CUTTING

If your design looks crooked or moved after cutting, it usually means the material shifted on the mat. Let's secure everything so your cuts stay where they're supposed to be.

1

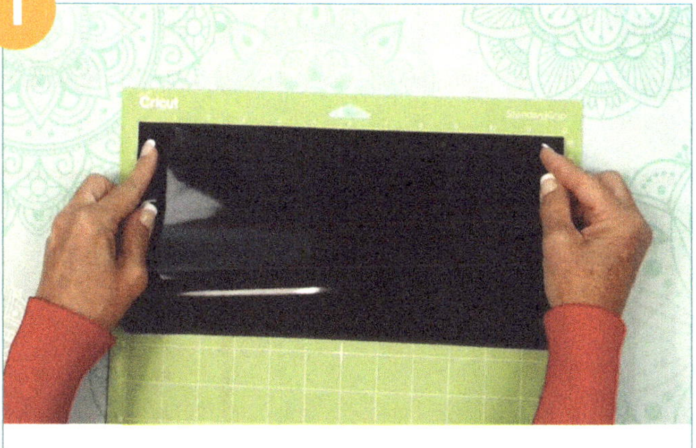

PRESS THE MATERIAL DOWN FLAT: Place your material on the mat and smooth it down firmly. Watch for bubbles, wrinkles, or edges lifting -- these can cause shifting during the cut. I recommend using a brayer if you have one.

2

CHECK MAT STICKINESS: Make sure your mat is sticky enough for the material you're using. If the mat feels worn, use a brayer or gently press the material down with your hands or replace the mat with a new one.

3

LOAD THE MAT STRAIGHT: Line the mat up with the guides on your Cricut and feed it in evenly. Push gently on the end of the mat so the mat touches the rollers evenly. If you are using an Explore, Maker, or Venture, press the Load/ Unload button. With the Joy or Joy Xtra, hold your material against the rollers -- the machine will pull it in.

4

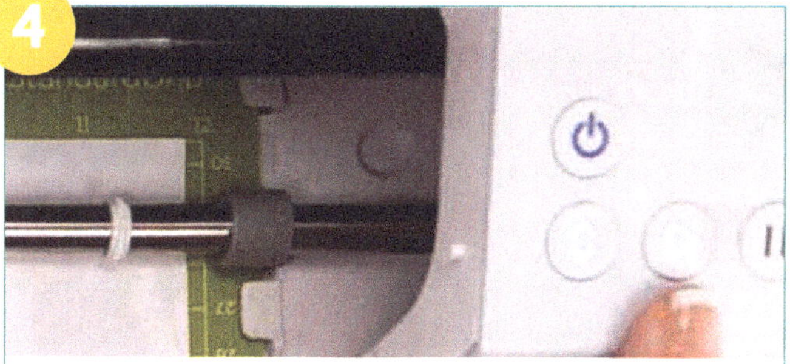

DO A SMALL TEST CUT: Before re-cutting your full design, try a small test shape to confirm everything stays in place.

MY CUT DOESN'T MATCH THE PREVIEW

The mat preview is meant to show exactly how your project will cut, so when the result doesn't match, it can be confusing. These steps help you catch the most common setup issues before cutting again.

1

CONFIRM YOU ARE CUTTING THE CORRECT PROJECT: Make sure you didn't accidentally edit or open a different version of your design. Small changes can affect how the cut looks.

2

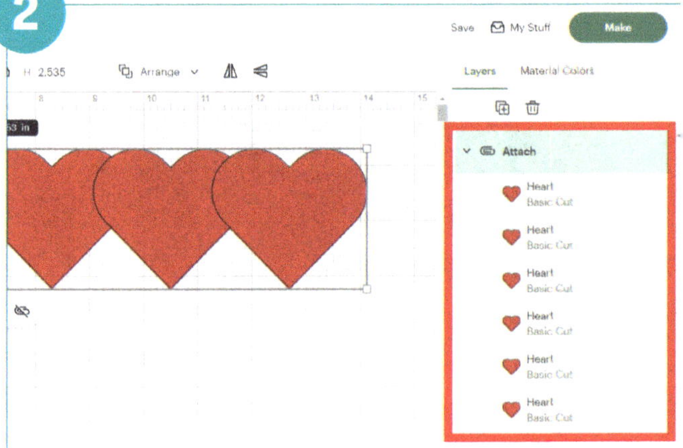

CHECK ATTACH, WELD, AND GROUPING: If you used Attach, Weld, or grouped layers, double-check that they're applied correctly. These settings control where designs cut on the mat.

3

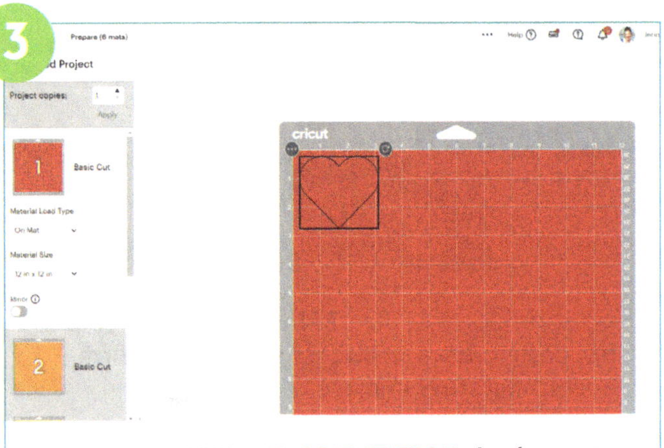

VERIFY MAT SIZE AND ORIENTATION: In the mat preview, confirm the mat size and orientation match the mat you loaded into the machine. A mismatch here can throw everything off.

4

CANCEL AND PREVIEW AGAIN: If something doesn't look right, cancel the cut and go back to the Canvas. Fix the issue and preview again before cutting.

MY CRICUT IS CUTTING SLOW

If your Cricut is creeping along, pausing constantly, or taking forever to finish a cut, your design is likely too complex for the size or material you're using. Slow cutting usually means the machine is following too many tiny cut paths. Let's speed things up.

1

ZOOM IN AND CHECK THE DETAILS: Zoom way in on your design and look for tiny shapes, rough edges, or extra points you don't actually need. If it looks busy up close, it will cut slowly.

2

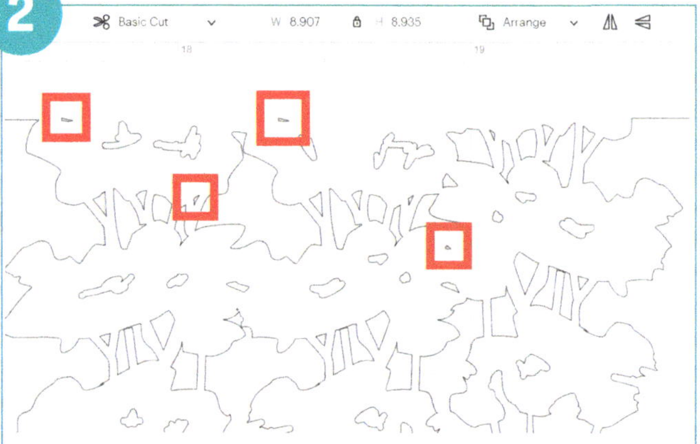

REMOVE OR SIMPLIFY THE DESIGN: Delete tiny cutouts, thin lines, or decorative details that won't be visible in the final project. Fewer paths = faster cutting.

3

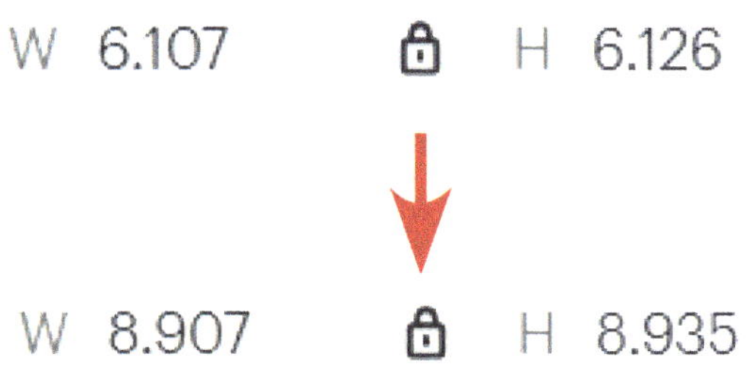

RESIZE THE DESIGN: Very small designs with lots of detail force the blade to make tiny, slow movements. Increasing the size slightly can dramatically improve cutting speed.

4

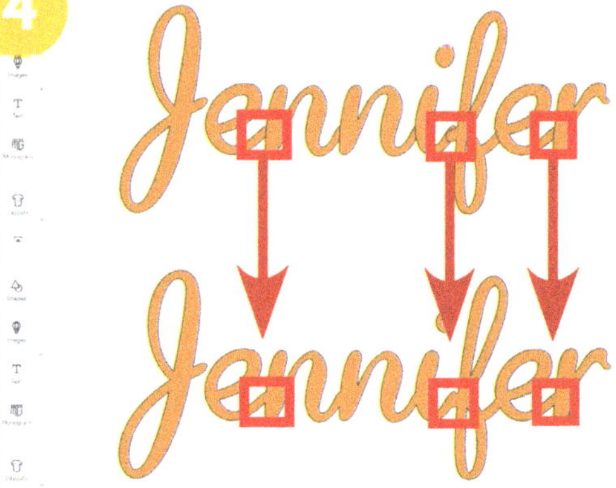

WELD WHERE SHAPES OVERLAP: If your design has overlapping shapes meant to be one piece, weld them. Welding reduces duplicate cut lines and helps the Cricut cut more efficiently.

TOO MANY LAYERS SLOWING DOWN YOUR CUT?

If your Cricut seems to pause between cuts or takes forever to finish, too many layers may be the culprit. Each layer adds more work for the machine. These steps help you streamline your project.

1

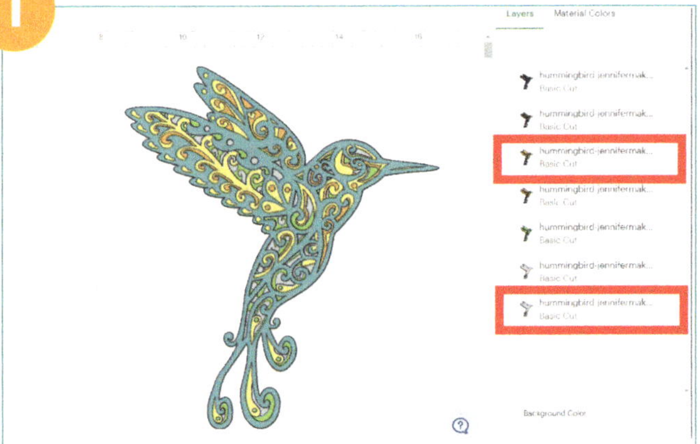

REVIEW THE LAYERS PANEL: Open the Layers panel and look for duplicate, hidden, or unnecessary layers that can be removed.

2

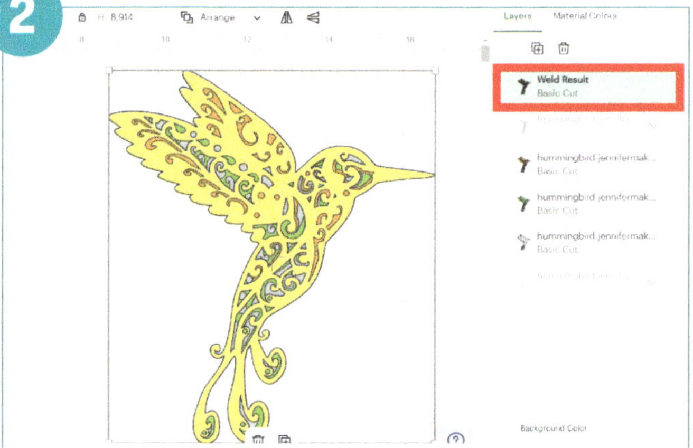

COMBINE LAYERS WHEN POSSIBLE: Weld shapes that should cut as one piece or attach items that need to stay together. Fewer layers mean faster cutting.

3

HIDE LAYERS YOU AREN'T CUTTING: Turn off visibility for layers you don't plan to cut right now by clicking the "eye" icon next to the layer. Design Space only processes visible layers.

4

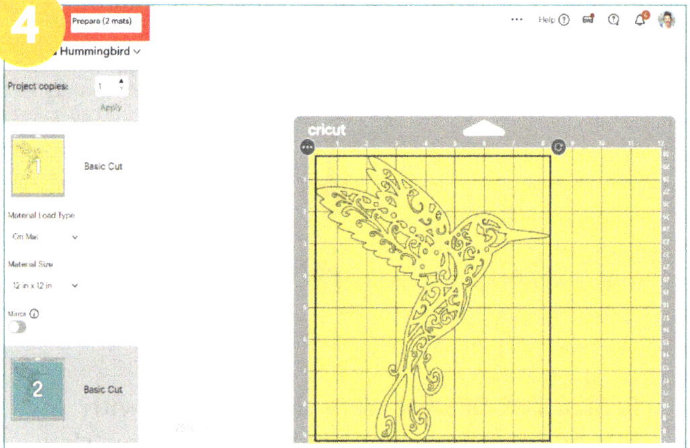

CUT IN SECTIONS: If your project has many parts, consider cutting it in smaller sections instead of all at once. Hide a couple layers and only cut one or two at a time.

DESIGN SPACE IS RUNNING SLOW

If Design Space feels slow, freezes, or doesn't respond the way it should, it doesn't mean your project is broken. Design Space can struggle when it's overloaded. These steps help it run more smoothly.

1

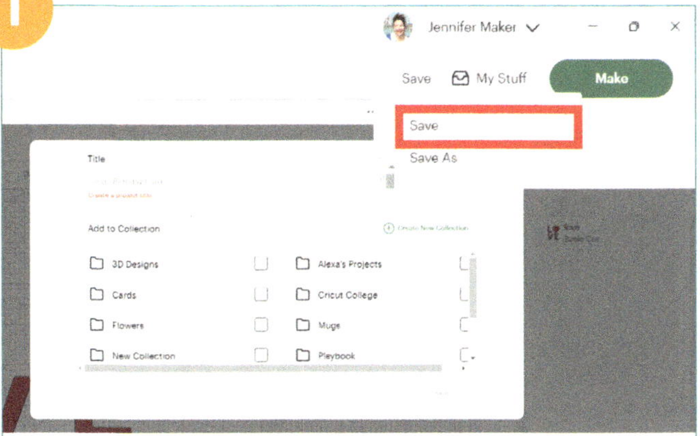

SAVE AND CLOSE THE PROJECT: Save your work and close Design Space completely. This clears temporary memory issues that can slow things down.

2

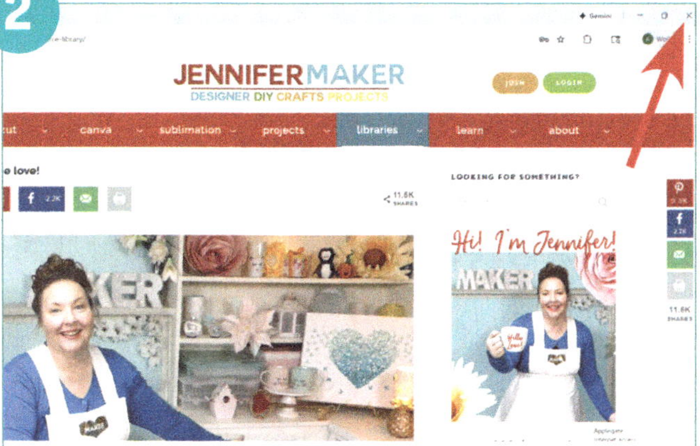

CLOSE OTHER PROGRAMS: Shut down other apps, browser tabs, or software running in the background. Design Space runs better when it has more system resources.

3

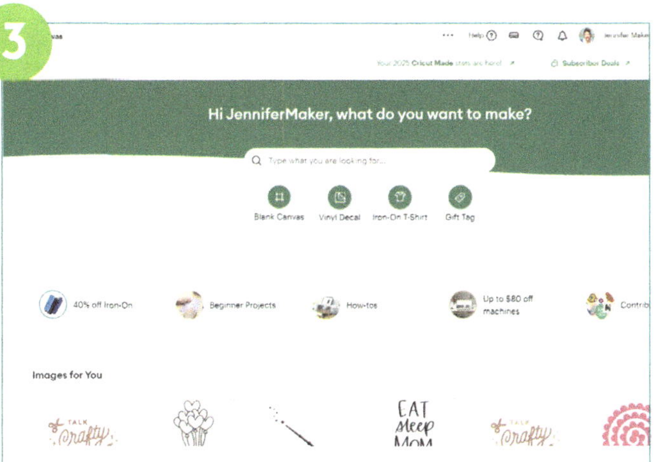

REOPEN DESIGN SPACE AND YOUR PROJECT: Reopen Design Space and load your project again. Many performance issues resolve after a fresh start.

4

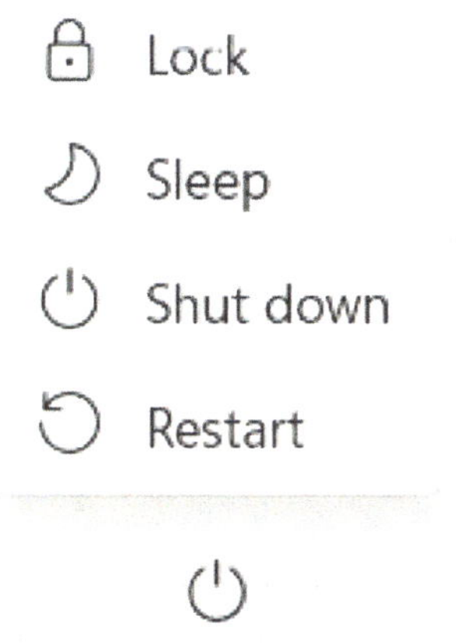

RESTART YOUR DEVICE IF NEEDED: If things are still laggy, restart your computer or mobile device before continuing.

BREAK BIG PROJECTS INTO SMALLER PARTS

Large or complex projects can overwhelm Design Space and slow everything down. Breaking a project into smaller pieces makes cutting faster and more reliable.

1

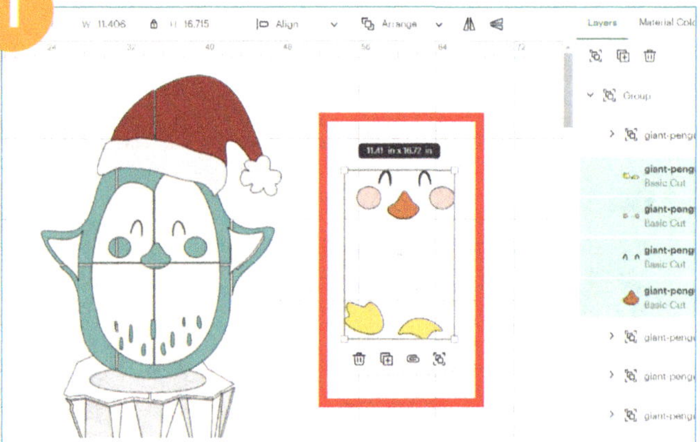

IDENTIFY CUTS THAT CAN BE SEPARATED: Look for parts of the design that can be cut separately without affecting the final result.

2

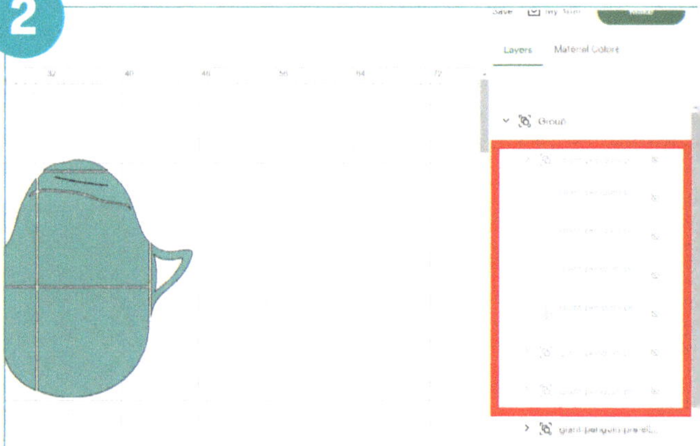

HIDE UNNEEDED LAYERS: Hide layers you aren't cutting right now. Design Space processes visible layers only. To hide a layer, click on it in the Layers Panel, then click the eye icon.

3

CUT ONE SECTION AT A TIME: Cut each section separately instead of all at once. This reduces processing load and cutting time.

4

ASSEMBLE AFTER CUTTING: Once all parts are cut, assemble them together as planned. The final result is the same -- just with less frustration.

REDUCE NODE OVERLOAD (WHEN POSSIBLE)

Nodes are the points that make up your design's cut paths. Too many nodes can slow cutting and cause lag. These steps help reduce unnecessary complexity.

1

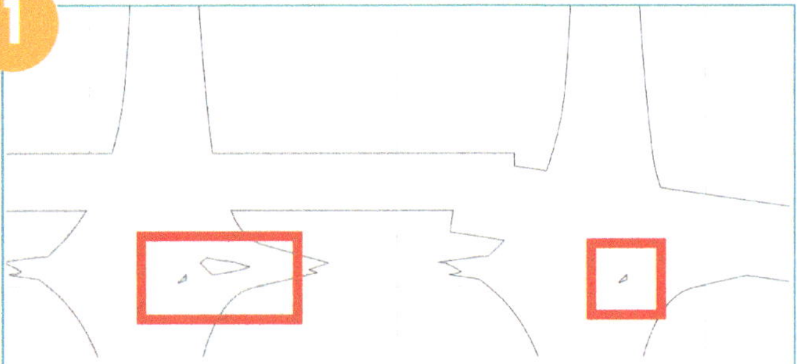

ZOOM IN TO SEE THE NODES: Zoom in closely on your design to spot rough edges, jagged lines, or tiny cuts caused by extra nodes.

2

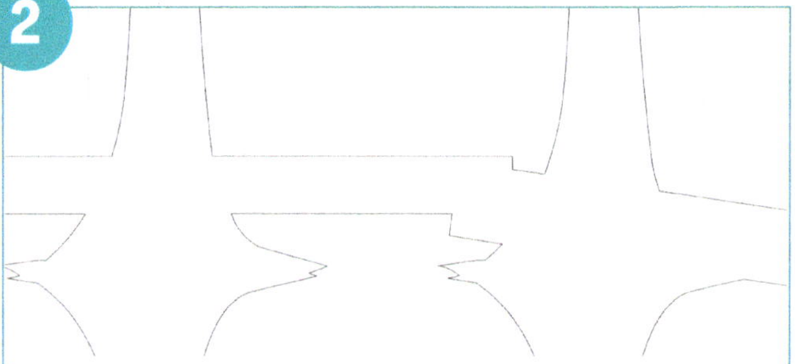

REMOVE UNNECESSARY DETAILS: Delete tiny shapes, decorative cuts, or fine details using the Contour, Slice, and/or Combine tools.

3

SIMPLIFY OR SMOOTH THE DESIGN: If possible, use simpler shapes or smoother versions of the design to reduce node count.

4

RESIZE TO REDUCE NODE DENSITY: Increasing the size of a very detailed design can help the Cricut cut more smoothly.

5

WELD WHERE SHAPES OVERLAP: Weld overlapping shapes that should be one piece. This removes duplicate cut lines and reduces nodes.

6

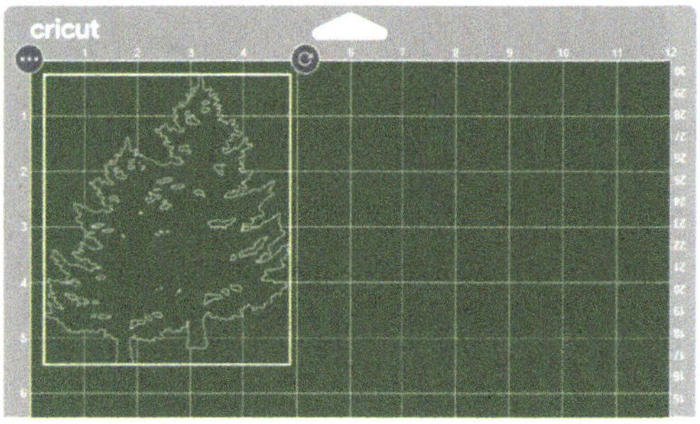

TEST CUT BEFORE FINAL PROJECT: Always test cut after simplifying to confirm the design cuts smoothly.

MAT NOT LOADING STRAIGHT

If your mat loads crooked or your cut starts in an odd spot, the mat likely wasn't aligned correctly when loading. A few small adjustments can make a big difference.

1

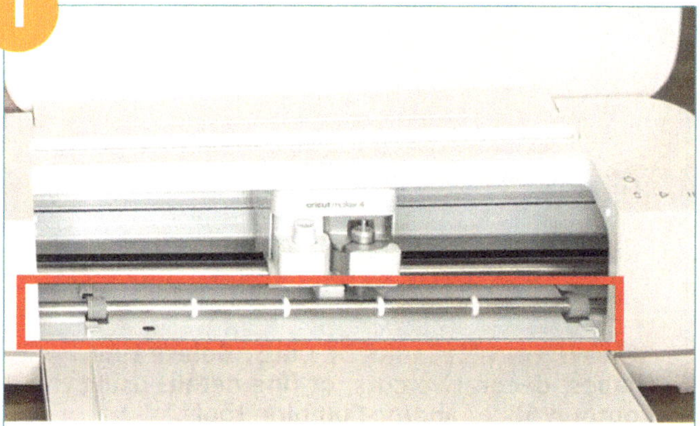

ALIGN THE MAT WITH THE GUIDES: Hold the mat flush against the guides on the Cricut. The edges should be straight and even before pressing the load button.

2

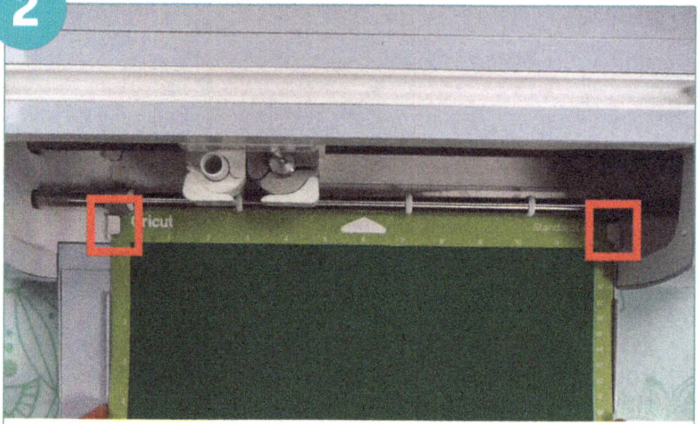

SUPPORT THE MAT WHILE LOADING: Keep the mat level with both hands as it feeds into the machine. Don't let it dip or tilt as it loads. Push the mat gently against the rollers before pressing the load button.

3

CHECK ROLLER AND MAT FOR DEBRIS: Look at the rollers and mat surface for small scraps or debris. Even tiny pieces can cause the mat to load unevenly.

4

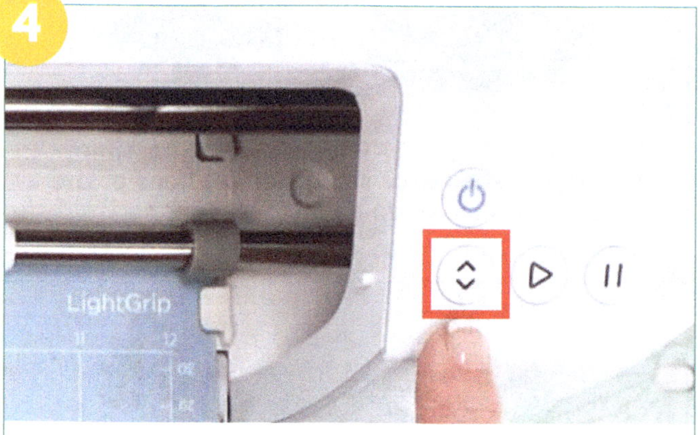

UNLOAD AND RELOAD MAT: If the mat doesn't look right, unload it and try again. Loading slowly and evenly usually fixes the problem.

CRICUT ISN'T CUTTING ALL THE WAY THROUGH

If your design didn't fully cut through the material, don't worry -- this is one of the most common Cricut issues. It usually just means a setting needs a small adjustment.

1

CONFIRM THE MATERIAL SETTINGS: Make sure the material selected in Design Space matches what you placed on the mat. The wrong material setting is the most common cause of incomplete cuts.

2

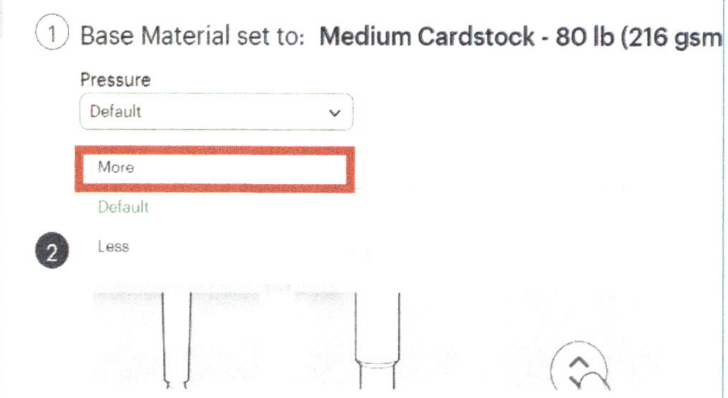

TRY MORE PRESSURE: If the material is correct, choose "More" from the Pressure drop-down menu and run the cut again. This increases how firmly the blade presses without changing the blade itself.

3

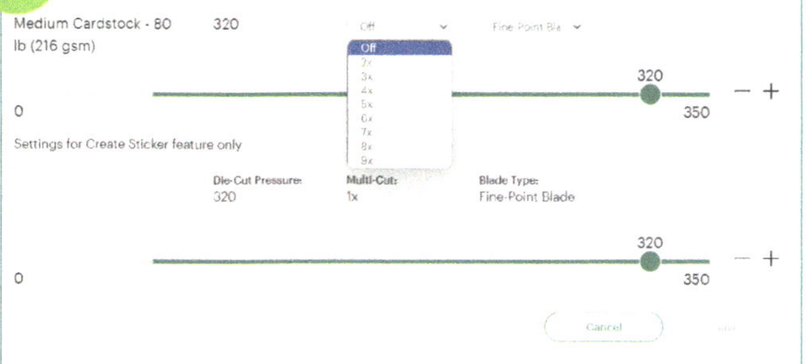

USE A SECOND PASS: For thicker or textured materials, enable a second pass instead of increasing pressure too much. Open "Settings," "Machines," and "Custom Materials." Click "Edit" next to the material you want to add a pass to. Under "Multi-cut" choose "2x."

4

CHECK BLADE AND MAT CONDITIONS: Check the blade for debris by pressing the plunger on the housing. While pressing the plunger, use an alcohol pad to clean any debris away. Make sure the material is firmly stuck to the mat.

NOTE: If more pressure and a second pass doesn't work, you may need to make a custom material with even more pressure.

WHY IS MY CRICUT OVERCUTTING?

If your material looks sliced too deeply or your cuts are going through the mat, the pressure is likely too high. Let's dial things back for cleaner results.

1

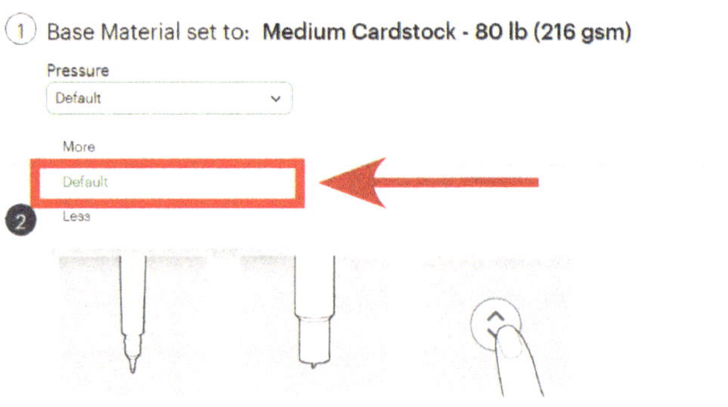

USE DEFAULT PRESSURE: Start by turning off More Pressure and returning to the Default setting. Too much pressure is the most common cause of overcutting.

2

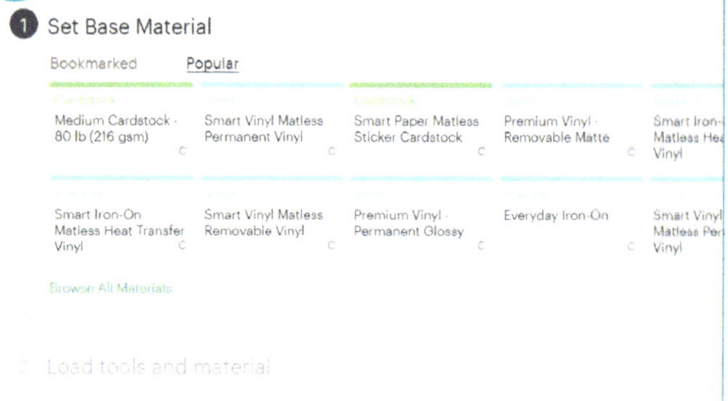

RECHECK THE MATERIAL SELECTION: Make sure you didn't accidentally select a heavier material than what you're cutting. Heavier settings use more pressure automatically.

3

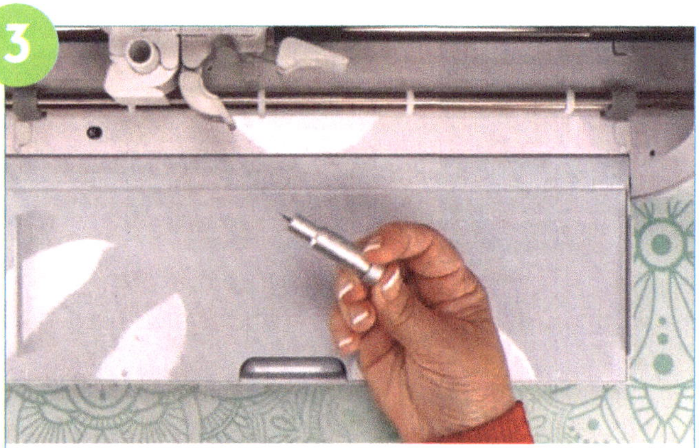

INSPECT THE BLADE: A damaged or improperly seated blade can cut deeper than expected. Remove the blade, reseat it inside the housing, and check for debris.

4

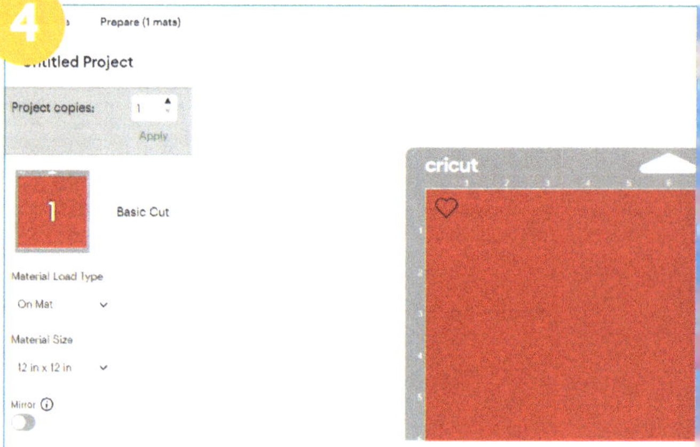

DO A TEST CUT: Before cutting the full design again, do a small test cut to confirm the pressure is just right.

NOTE: Be sure you are using a "Premium" blade (not a "Standard" blade). Some older Cricut blades meant for other machines are a little different and can cause this issue.

MATERIAL IS DRAGGING OR TEARING

Dragging or tearing usually means the material isn't staying flat during the cut. The good news? This is almost always an easy fix.

1

SECURE THE MATERIAL FLAT: Press the material down firmly on the mat using a brayer, especially around edges and corners. Any lifting can cause tearing.

2

CHECK THE MAT STICKINESS: Make sure you're using the correct mat and that it's still sticky enough. A worn mat allows material to move during cutting, but a sticky mat will hold the material in place. You may need to clean your mat to get it sticky again. Get directions at jennifermaker.com/how-to-clean-cricut-mat.

3

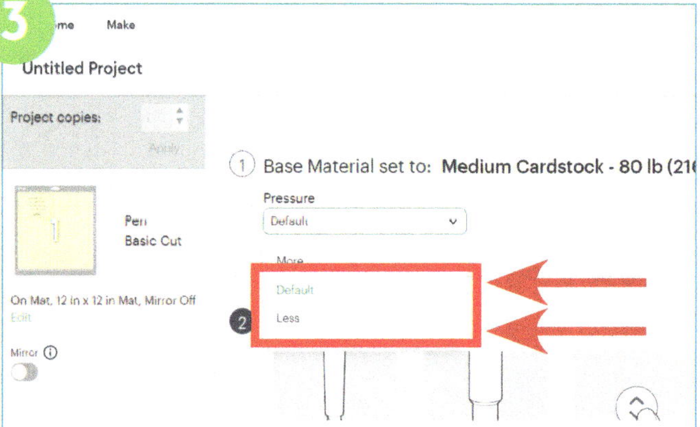

REDUCE PRESSURE IF NEEDED: Too much pressure can cause the blade to drag through the material instead of slicing cleanly. Try Default or Less Pressure if tearing continues.

4

WATCH THE FIRST FEW CUTS: Stay nearby during the start of the cut. If you see dragging or lifting, pause the cut and adjust before continuing.

BLADE DEPTH VS PRESSURE: WHAT'S THE DIFFERENCE?

This is a super common point of confusion, so you're not alone! Cricut machines automatically control blade depth. When cuts aren't clean, the adjustment you want is usually pressure — not the blade.

1

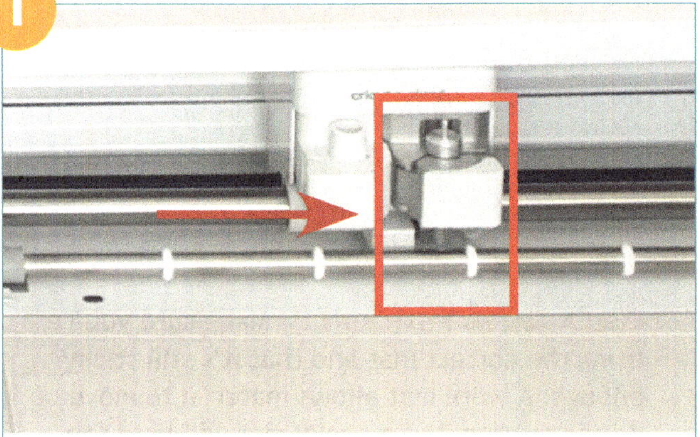

KNOW THAT BLADE DEPTH IS AUTOMATIC: Cricut blades are designed to self-adjust. You don't manually change how far the blade sticks out of the housing.

2

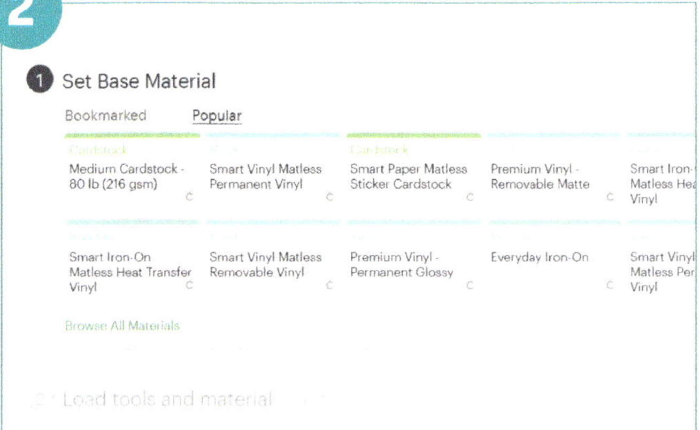

USE MATERIAL SETTINGS TO CONTROL PRESSURE: The material you choose in Design Space tells the machine how much pressure to apply. Always start with the correct material.

3

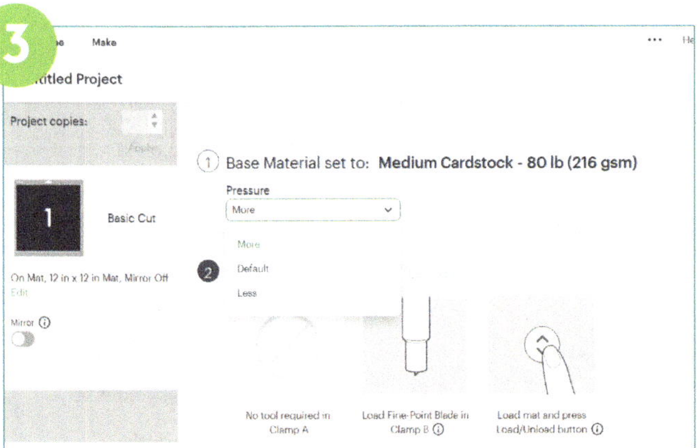

ADJUST PRESSURE, NOT THE BLADE: If cuts aren't right, try changing the Pressure or a second pass instead of changing blades or blade housings.

4

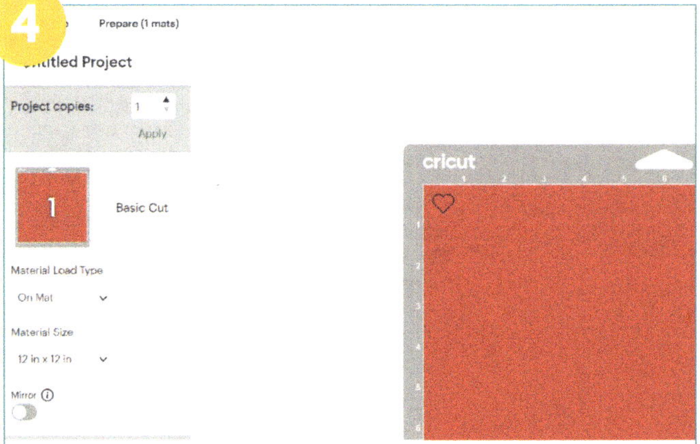

TEST CUT BEFORE CUTTING THE WHOLE DESIGN: A quick test cut helps you find the sweet spot without wasting materials.

MATERIAL-SPECIFIC TROUBLESHOOTING

- Cardstock is Tearing
- Cardstock is Curling
- Cardstock Has Frayed or Fuzzy Edges
- Best Cardstock Settings to Try First
- Vinyl is Not Sticking to the Mat
- Weeding Tips and Tricks
- Cuts Are Too Deep or Not Deep Enough
- Transfer Tape Issues
- Mirroring Mistakes
- Iron-On Vinyl Peeling After Pressing
- Iron-On VInyl Not Adhering at All
- Iron-On Vinyl Layering Issues
- Glitter Vinyl Tips and Tricks
- Foil and Holographic Vinyl Tips and Tricks
- Faux Leather Tips and Tricks
- Printable Materials Tips and Tricks
- Forgetting Stabilizer for Fabric
- Basswood or Veneer Chipping or Cracking

CARDSTOCK IS TEARING

Is your cardstock tearing when your Cricut cuts it? Is it tearing when you try to remove it from the mat, with parts remaining stuck to the mat? Here's how to avoid these things.

1

USE A LIGHTGRIP OR STANDARDGRIP MAT: Purple StrongGrip mats grab some cardstock fibers too aggressively, especially thin or smooth papers, which causes the cardstock to rip.

2

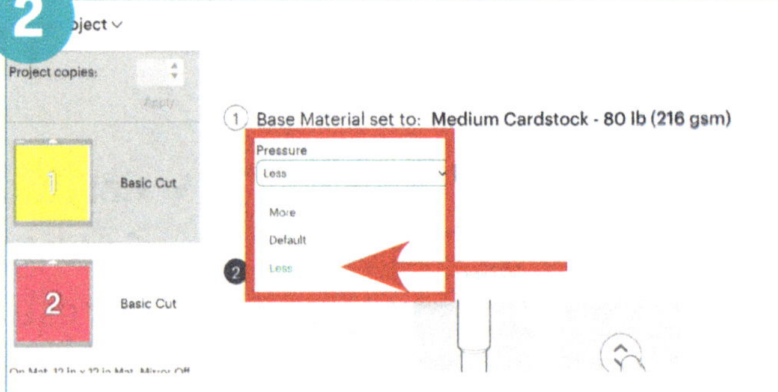

REDUCE CUTTING PRESSURE: Too much pressure causes the blade to drag instead of slice cleanly, so try using the "Less" Pressure setting.

3

USE A FINE-POINT BLADE: The Deep-Point Blade and Knife Blade are too aggressive for paper and cardstock and increase tearing.

4

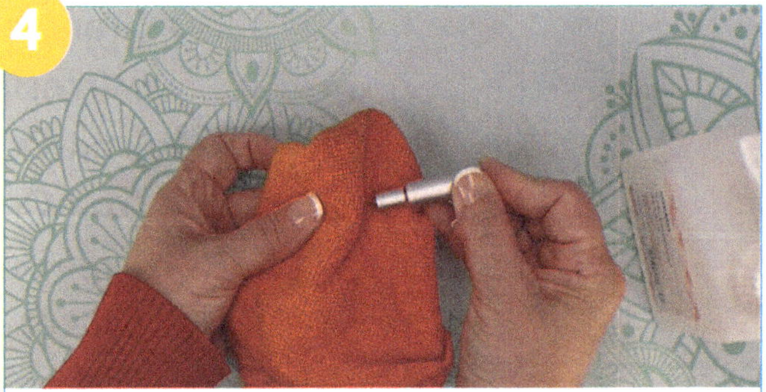

CHECK BLADE: Use rubbing alcohol and a micro-fiber cloth to clean the blade.

5

TAPE CARDSTOCK EDGES WITH PAINTER'S TAPE: This prevents lifting during cuts. Only tape the edges of the cardstock where your Cricut won't cut and away from the rollers that draw in the mat. Be sure that the tape does not wrap around the edges of the mat.

6

PLACE TEXTURED CARDSTOCK FACE DOWN: Cutting from the smooth side down into the textured side produces cleaner edges. Just remember to mirror your design for this!

CARDSTOCK IS CURLING

Sometimes cardstock curls up off of the mat, making cutting difficult. Other times, your cardstock starts curling as you remove it from the mat. Here's how to avoid both of these situations or solve the problems you're already experiencing.

1

DE-STICK THE MAT SLIGHTLY: Overly sticky mats curl cardstock when removed, so de-stick the mat a little by pressing it against your shirt or another fabric surface.

2

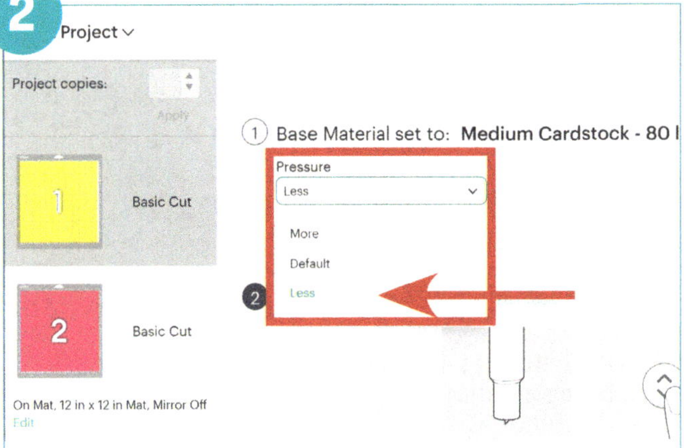

REDUCE CUTTING PRESSURE: Try cutting with the "Default" or even "Less" pressure setting. This reduces stress on paper fibers during cutting.

3

PEEL THE MAT AWAY: Flip the mat over and slowly peel it away from the cardstock instead of peeling the cardstock up off of the mat. This keeps paper flat.

4

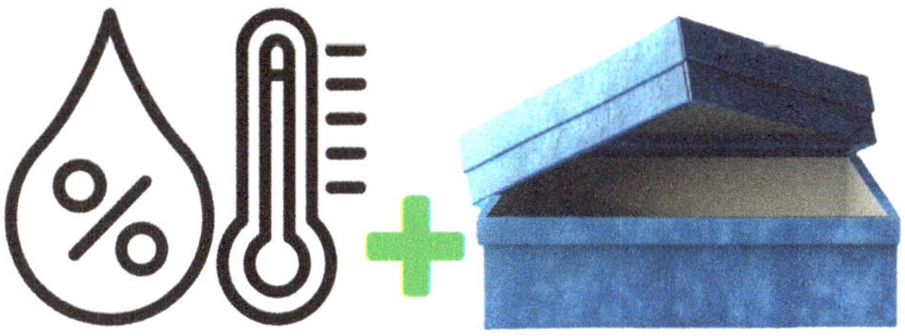

CONTROL HUMIDITY: Moist, warm air causes cardstock to warp before and after cutting, so keep cardstock in closed containers in a controlled, cool environment. If you suspect that your cardstock is damp, use an EasyPress on low to reduce moisture.

CARDSTOCK HAS FRAYED OR FUZZY EDGES

Does your cardstock have frayed or fuzzy edges where your Cricut cut it? This can be frustrating because it ruins the sharp, well-defined edges of a project. Let's fix that.

1

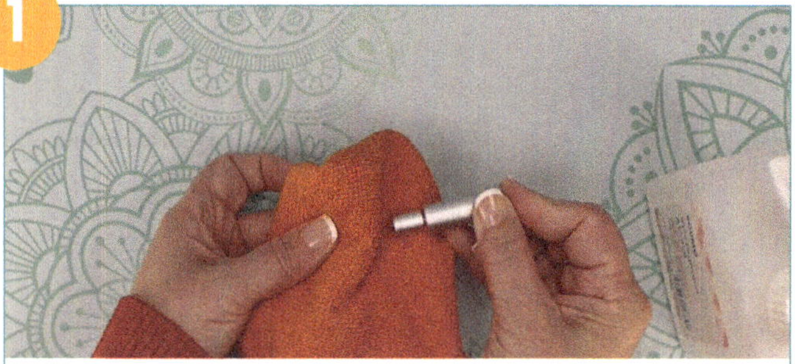

CHECK BLADE: Try cleaning it carefully with rubbing alcohol and a microfiber cloth. Be careful – the blade is sharp!

2

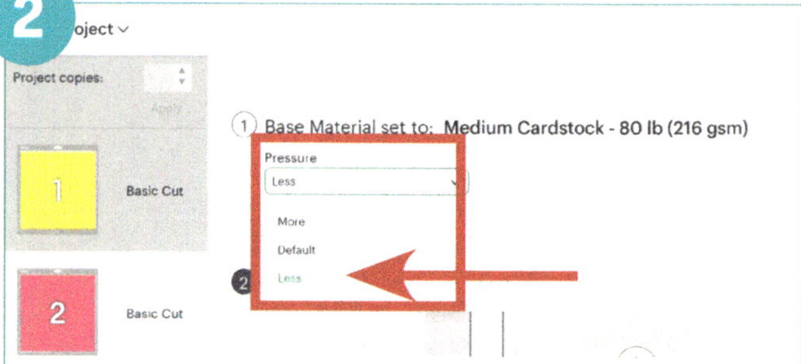

REDUCE CUTTING PRESSURE: Try cutting with the "Default" or even "Less" pressure setting. This reduces stress on paper fibers during cutting.

3

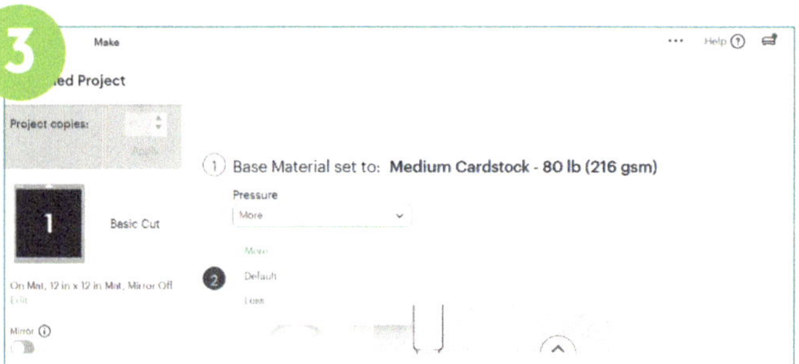

USE THE "CARDSTOCK FOR INTRICATE CUTS" SETTING: This setting slows down the cut and adjusts the pressure automatically.

4

CUT TEXTURED CARDSTOCK FACE DOWN: Fibers can tear unevenly on small, detailed designs, and both embossed and debossed cardstock. Don't forget to mirror if cutting face down.

5

SECURE PAPER WITH A BRAYER: Once you've put your cardstock on the mat, firmly roll over it with a brayer to make sure it's adhered well.

6

MATCH PAPER TO PROJECT: Ultra-fine cuts don't suit all types, like glitter cardstock, embossed or debossed cardstock, and some foil cardstocks.

BEST CARDSTOCK SETTINGS TO TRY FIRST

Are you unsure what cardstock cut and pressure settings to use with different types of cardstock? Is your cardstock not cutting right with the setting you're using? Try the settings below.

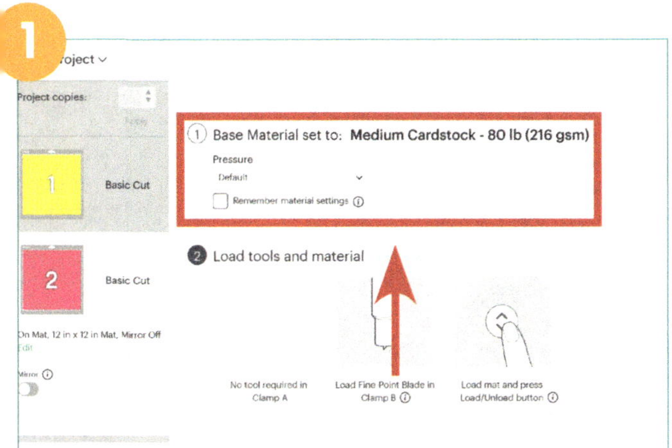

MEDIUM CARDSTOCK WITH MORE PRESSURE: This is the most reliable baseline setting for me across all machines. Medium cardstock weight is usually 80 to 100 pounds.

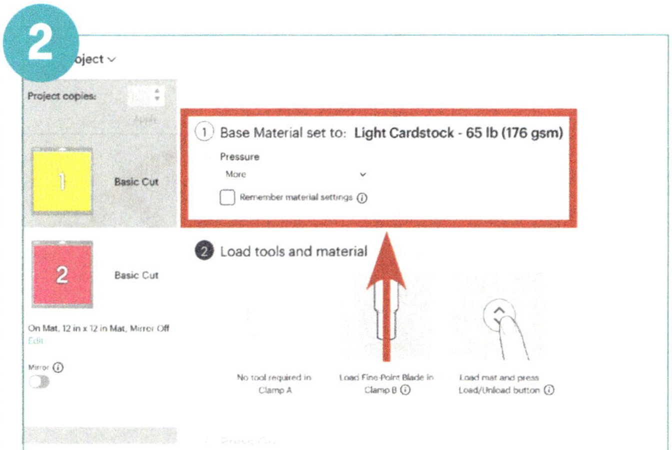

LIGHT CARDSTOCK WITH MORE PRESSURE: This setting is useful for thin cardstock that isn't cutting all the way through. Light cardstock weight is usually 65 to 80 pounds.

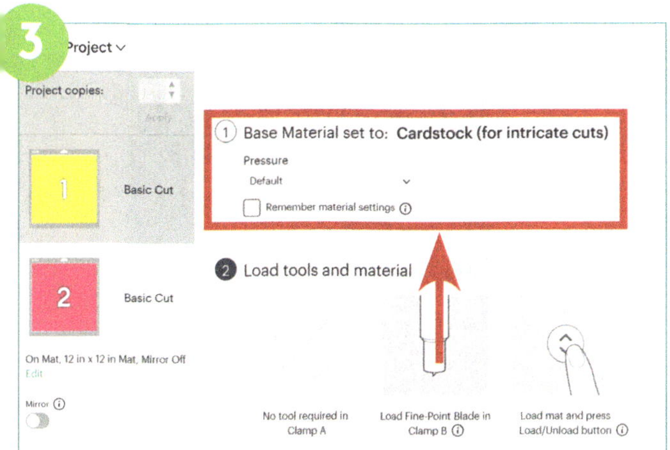

CARDSTOCK FOR INTRICATE CUTS: This is usually the best setting for cardstock projects with small text, lace, and super-detailed and delicate designs.

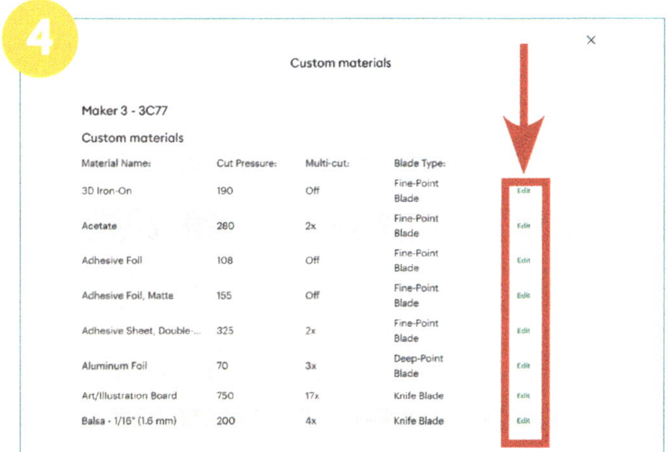

CUSTOM MATERIAL ADJUSTMENTS: In the Settings menu, choose "Machines" and "Custom Materials." Click "Edit" to change pressure or create your own custom material setting.

VINYL IS NOT STICKING TO THE MAT

There are several reasons why your vinyl is not sticking to the mat. The mat could be dirty or not strong enough. Vinyl that was stored rolled up often is stubborn and doesn't lay flat on a mat. Here's how to address these issues.

1

USE A GREEN STANDARDGRIP MAT: The LightGrip mat is often not sticky enough for vinyl, and the StrongGrip mat is too sticky for most vinyl (there are some exceptions), so use the green StandardGrip mat most of the time.

2

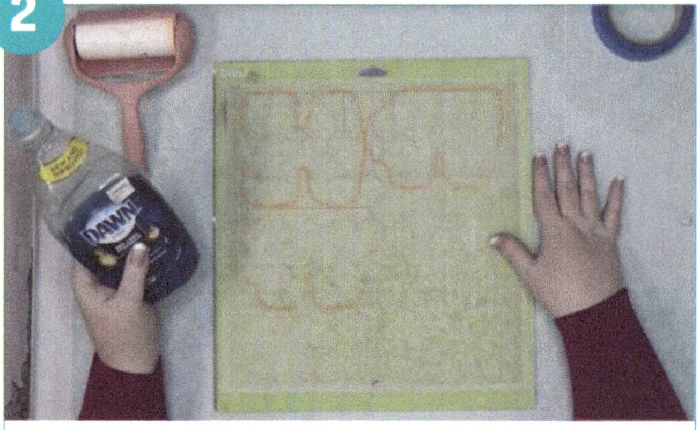

CLEAN THE MAT: Dust and debris reduce adhesion quickly. I just use alcohol-free baby wipes or Dawn dish soap and a gentle sponge, then let my mat air dry. It will magically be sticky again!

3

BRAYER VINYL DOWN FIRMLY: Once the vinyl is on a mat, roll a brayer all over it. This ensures full contact with the mat surface and helps keep the vinyl from curling up at the edges.

4

TAPE CURLED EDGES: Use painter's tape to tape down the edges of curling vinyl. Keep the tape away from where the Cricut will cut and where the gray rollers will draw the mat in.

WEEDING TIPS AND TRICKS

Weeding can be a difficult and frustrating process, but it doesn't have to be that way! Here are some tips and tricks for making the weeding easier and a little quicker, too.

1

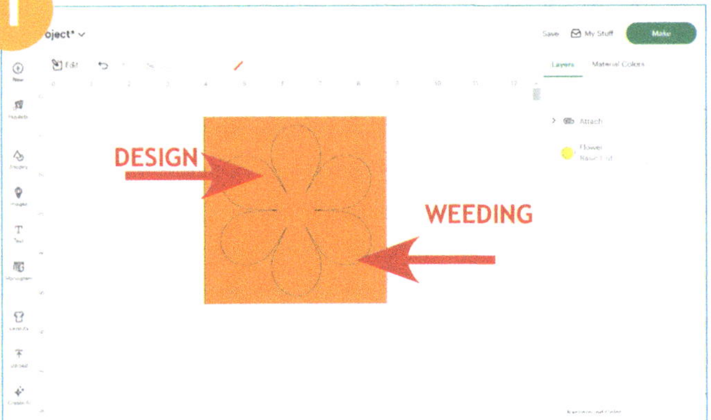

ADD WEEDING BOXES: Attach a square or rectangle of the same color as a design element to add a weeding box around your design. This reduces the amount of vinyl you're weeding away all at once.

2

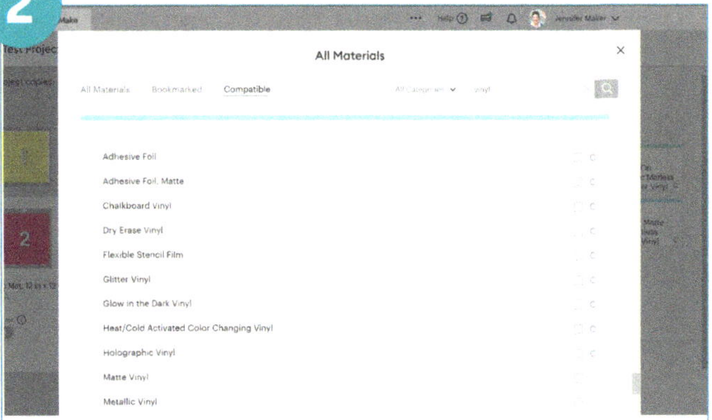

USE THE PROPER VINYL SETTING: The wrong material settings cause cut issues, so match your vinyl setting to the type of vinyl you're using. Access different materials on the Materials screen by clicking "Browse All Materials."

3

START WEEDING FROM THE OUTSIDE: Always start weeding your vinyl design from the outside and work your way in towards the middle of the design. This helps keep small details anchored longer.

4

TRY REVERSE WEEDING: Try applying the transfer tape first, then weeding away the excess vinyl off of the transfer tape. This can be helpful when you have a lot of small or thin details. Get help at jennifermaker.com/reverse-weed-vinyl.

CUTS ARE TOO DEEP OR NOT DEEP ENOUGH

Are you struggling to get the right cut depth for your vinyl? Maybe the vinyl isn't being cut all the way through, or maybe the cuts are so deep that the carrier sheet gets cut through, too? Here's how to approach these problems.

1

VERIFY BLADE TYPE: The Premium Fine-Point blade is the correct blade for most vinyl. Do not use the Deep-Point Blade or Knife Blade unless Design Space specifically calls for it during the Make process.

2

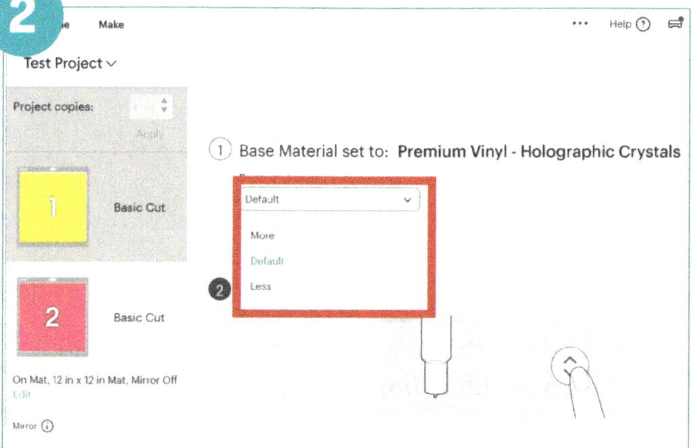

ADJUST PRESSURE BEFORE CHANGING BLADES: If your cuts aren't deep enough, try the "More" Pressure setting. If your cuts are too deep, try the "Default" or "Less" Pressure settings.

3

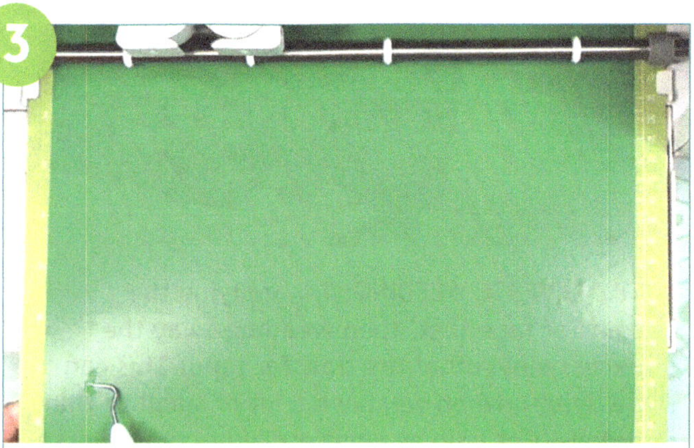

ALWAYS RUN A TEST CUT: Vinyl brands vary in thickness, even if two brands say they are the same. If you're using a new brand of vinyl, run a test cut on a small piece.

4

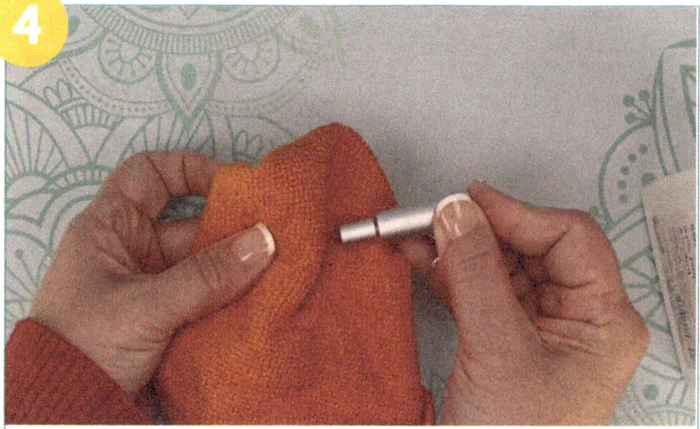

CLEAN YOUR BLADE: Try cleaning your blade (still in the housing) by using an alcohol pad or rubbing alcohol on a micro-fiber cloth.

TRANSFER TAPE ISSUES

Transfer tape is used to move a design cut from either permanent or removable vinyl off of its carrier sheet and onto the item you want it to be on. If you're having issues using transfer tape, try the tips below.

1

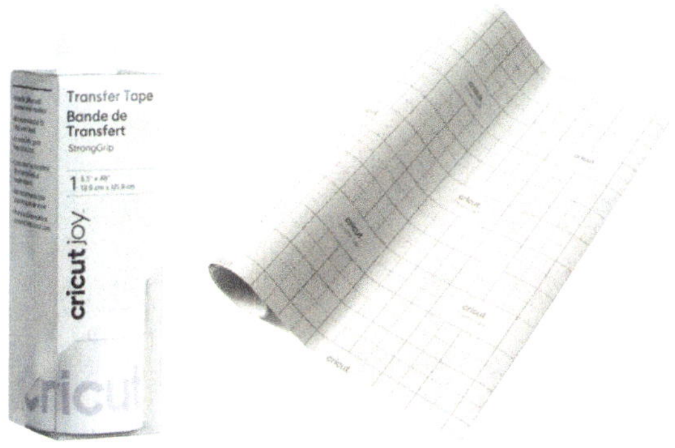

USE THE CORRECT TAPE STRENGTH: For most vinyl, you'll want to use regular StandardGrip transfer tape. If you're using glitter or shimmer vinyl, try using the StrongGrip transfer tape because the glitter vinyl's surface is rougher.

2

BURNISH TAPE AFTER APPLYING: After you apply transfer tape to your cut vinyl, firmly press over it with a brayer or scraper tool. This helps lift the design cleanly.

3

DE-STICK TAPE THAT IS TOO STICKY: Try pressing your transfer tape against a lint-free microfiber cloth a few times to decrease the stickiness. You can also try painter's tape or Press 'n' Seal.

4

SLOWLY PEEL THE CARRIER SHEET AWAY: Peel the carrier sheet away slowly and at a 45 degree angle. If pieces don't transfer, put the carrier sheet back down and burnish it again.

MIRRORING MISTAKES

It happens to everyone: you create a beautiful design, cut it out, and then when you prepare to press it, you discover that it's backwards and you forgot to mirror. Here's how to avoid that mistake.

1

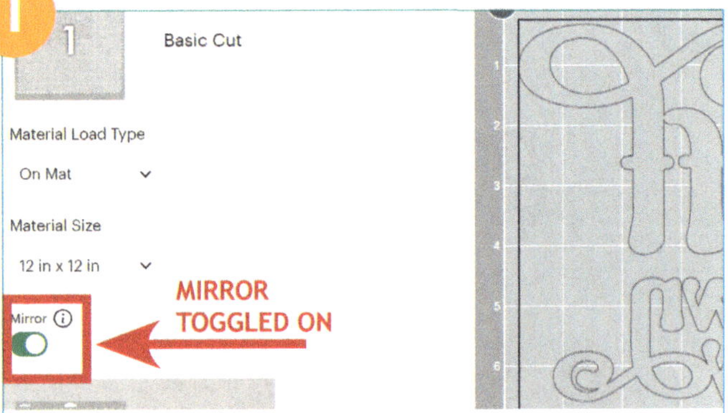

MIRROR MOST IRON-ON DESIGNS: Iron-on vinyl is cut from the back, so mirroring makes sure your design reads correctly once pressed. Most solid, glitter, foil, holographic, puff, flocked, and glow-in-the-dark iron-on vinyl all need mirrored.

2

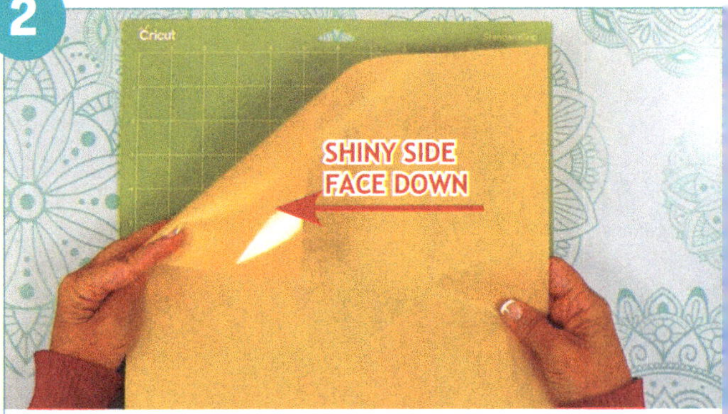

PLACE VINYL SHINY SIDE DOWN ON THE MAT: The shiny carrier sheet protects your design and keeps all the pieces in place while cutting, while exposing the vinyl itself to your Cricut's cutting blade.

3

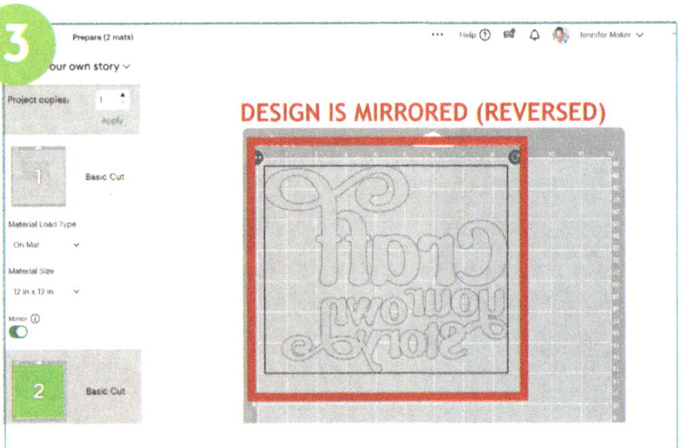

CHECK THE PREVIEW SCREEN: Look at your preview screen to confirm that your design is mirrored. This is your last chance to catch a backward design, so always take a quick look.

4

MAKE MIRRORING A HABIT: Always ask yourself, "Did I turn the Mirror function on?" I even have some fun Print Then Cut stickers you can put on your Cricut to help you remember to mirror at jennifermaker.com/cricut-for-beginners.

IRON-ON VINYL PEELING AFTER PRESSING

Is your iron-on vinyl peeling up after you've pressed it with a home iron or heat press? There are steps you can take to help prevent this from happening.

1

INCREASE PRESS TIME: Under-pressing is the most common reason iron-on peels, so adding a few extra seconds to your press time often fixes it.

2

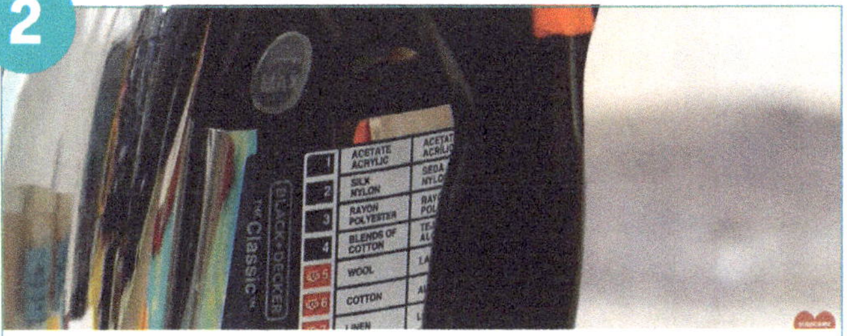

DOUBLE-CHECK THE TEMPERATURE: Home irons can run cooler than expected, so make sure yours is hot enough. If you have a heat press with a digital display, use it.

3

USE FIRM, EVEN PRESSURE: Don't be afraid to press down with some of your body weight. If using a household iron, don't use steam.

4

PEEL AS INSTRUCTED: Some iron-on vinyl needs you to peel the carrier sheet away while warm, while others need to wait until it has cooled off.

5

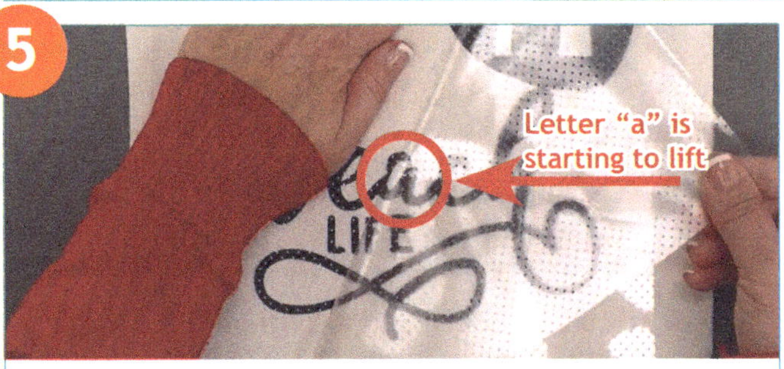

REPRESSING: If you've peeled the carrier sheet away but the vinyl isn't adhered well enough, place the carrier sheet back down and press again.

6

WAIT 24 HOURS BEFORE WASHING: Giving the adhesive time to cure helps your design last much longer, so don't wash your clothing item with a vinyl design right away.

IRON-ON VINYL NOT ADHERING AT ALL

Are you having trouble getting your iron-on vinyl to stick to your fabric? It happens, but don't worry, because it's usually very easy to fix!

1

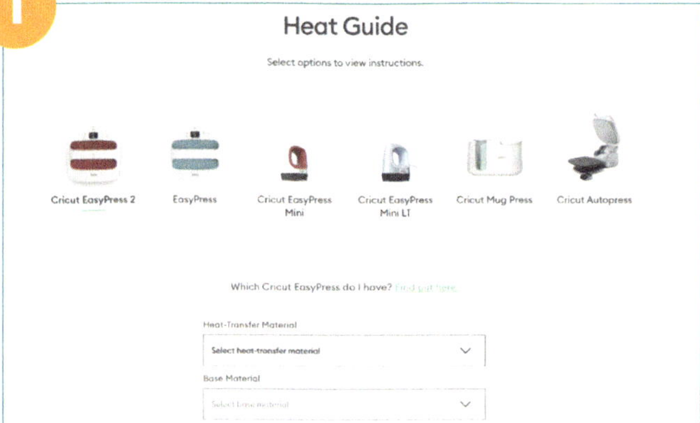

CONFIRM THE CORRECT HEAT SETTING: Each iron-on type and brand has its own temperature needs. Check the manufacturer's instructions. If there are no manufacturer instructions, use the Cricut Heat Guide at cricut.com/heatguide.

2

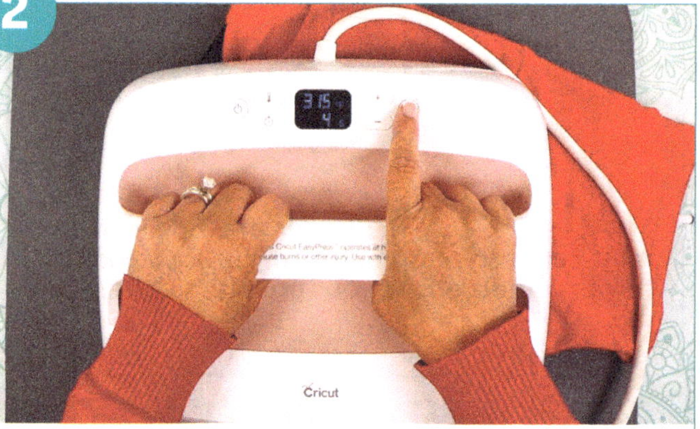

LINT ROLL AND PREHEAT YOUR FABRIC: Before applying iron-on vinyl, remove loose fibers with a lint roller, then use your iron or heat press to quickly press your fabric for 5 to 10 seconds to remove moisture and wrinkles.

3

APPLY PROPER PRESSURE: Light pressure won't activate the adhesive on iron-on vinyl. Firm pressure is best, so don't be afraid to really press down with some of your body weight.

4

TEST THE PEEL BEFORE REMOVING THE CARRIER: If edges of the iron-on vinyl begin to lift when you peel up the carrier sheet, lay the carrier sheet back down and press again right away.

IRON-ON VINYL LAYERING ISSUES

Is your vinyl not sticking when you're pressing a layered design? Are lower layers melting or scorching when you press a new layer? There's a solution for these problems!

1

BRIEFLY TACK LOWER LAYERS: Only press each lower layer for 5-10 seconds, which is just long enough to tack it down.

2

REMOVE THE CARRIER SHEET: Peel the carrier sheet away slowly and at an angle. This creates a smooth surface for your next layer.

3

LINE UP LAYERS CAREFULLY: Small shifts can really stand out once everything is pressed, so take your time lining your design layers up before pressing.

4

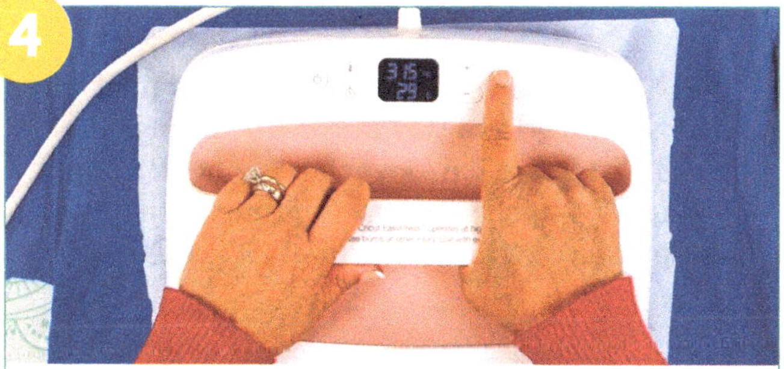

COVER THE LAYERS: Lay a sheet of parchment or white uncoated butcher paper over the design each time you tack down a layer. This protects exposed vinyl from heat damage.

5

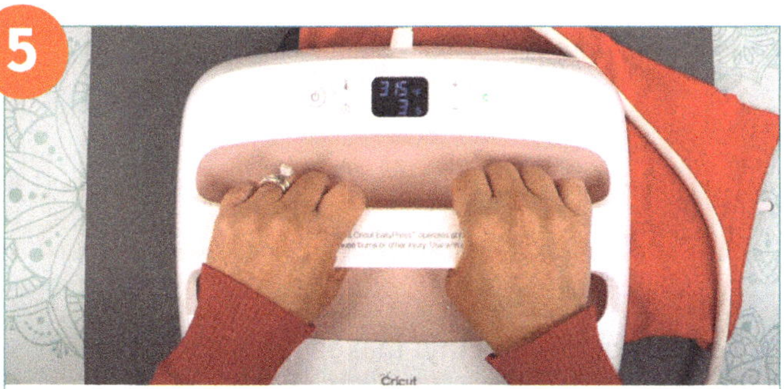

FINISH WITH A FULL PRESS: When adhering the top layer of your design, press for the full recommended amount of time. This bonds all layers together evenly.

6

AVOID GLITTER AS A BASE LAYER: The texture of glitter vinyl makes it hard for other layers to stick. Only use it as a top layer in your designs.

GLITTER IRON-ON VINYL TIPS AND TRICKS

Glitter vinyl is bold, sparkly, and a total show-stopper, but it does have a few quirks that can surprise even experienced crafters. Here's how to work with those quirks.

1

USE A STRONGGRIP MAT: Glitter vinyl is thick and needs extra grip to stay put when cutting, so place glitter iron-on vinyl on a StrongGrip mat and use a brayer to adhere it firmly to the mat. Use painter's tape on the edges, if necessary.

2

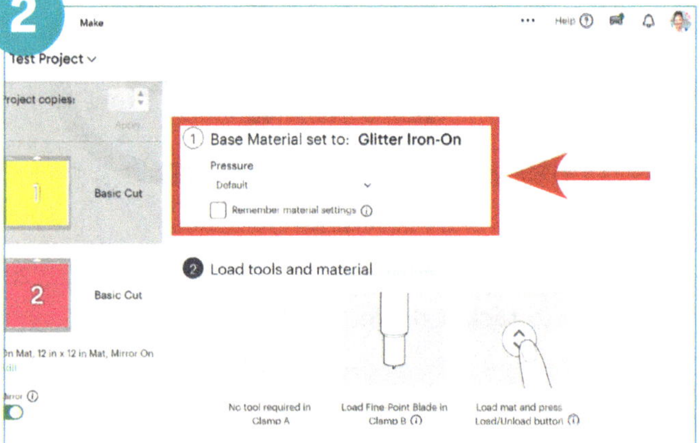

USE THE "GLITTER IRON-ON" SETTING: When preparing your cut in Design Space, select the "Glitter Vinyl" cut setting. This automatically adjusts the cut depth and strength for thicker material.

3

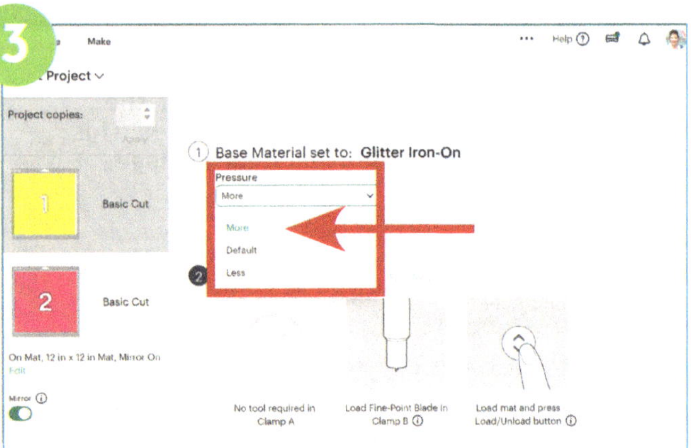

INCREASE PRESSURE: Glitter iron-on vinyl is thicker than standard iron-on vinyl, and some brands are thicker than others. Try using the "More" Pressure setting along with the "Glitter Iron-On" material setting.

4

DON'T LAYER ON TOP OF GLITTER VINYL: The texture of glitter vinyl makes it hard for other layers to stick, so only use it as a top layer in your designs.

FOIL AND HOLOGRAPHIC VINYL TIPS AND TRICKS

Foil and holographic iron-on vinyl are absolutely gorgeous, but they're also some of the most finicky materials to work with. Here are some adjustments you can make to help make these materials easier to work with.

1

USE A STANDARDGRIP MAT: Use a green StandardGrip mat for foil and holographic iron-on vinyl. Avoid using a purple StrongGrip mat because too strong of a grip can dent or crack foil and holographic surfaces.

2

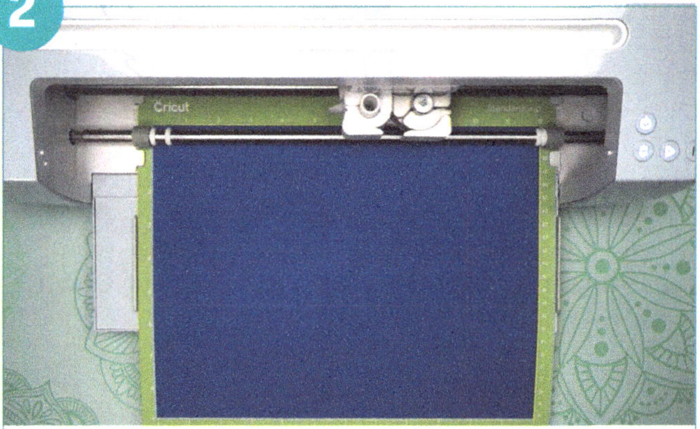

DO A TEST CUT: Foil iron-on vinyl can tear if cut too deeply, while holographic iron-on vinyl may need slightly more pressure. Always do a test cut with a scrap or small piece of the vinyl you are using.

3

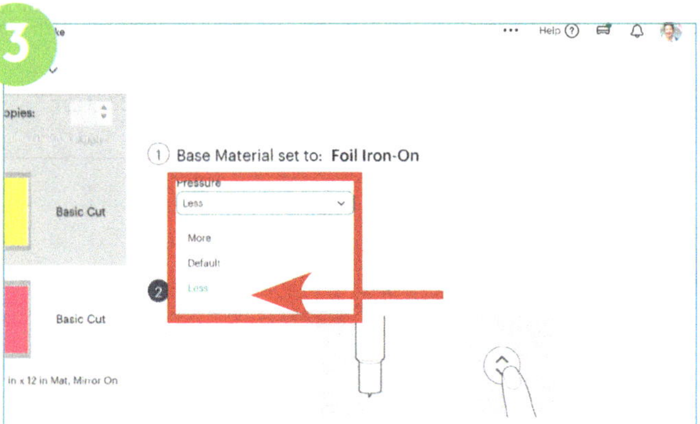

LOWER PRESSURE IF FOIL CRACKS: Foil layers are thin and can split if over-cut, so if this happens, try decreasing the pressure setting to "Less."

4

PEEL PROPERLY: Peel the carrier sheet away slowly and at a sharp angle. This protects the vinyl and keeps edges smooth. Foil and holographic iron-on vinyl can also wrinkle if the carrier sheet is removed too quickly.

FAUX LEATHER TIPS AND TRICKS

Faux leather is a great material for earrings, keychains, and home decor, but only when it's cut the right way. Here's how to prevent tearing, dragging, and uneven cuts.

1

USE A STRONGGRIP MAT: Faux leather is heavy and needs a strong hold, so use a purple StrongGrip mat when cutting it with your Cricut.

2

TAPE DOWN THE EDGES: Use painter's tape to hold the edges of the faux leather down on the mat to prevent shifting while cutting. Don't put tape where your design will cut.

3

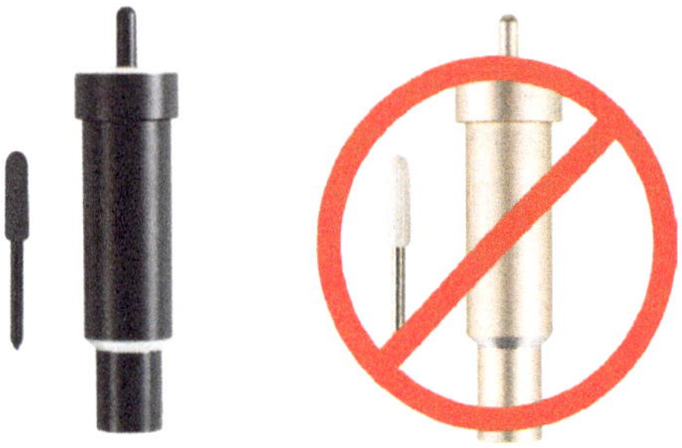

USE THE RIGHT BLADE: Thicker materials need a stronger blade, so try using the Deep-Point Blade instead of the Fine-Point Blade.

4

USE THE RIGHT SETTING: The slower cut speed and higher pressure level of the "Faux Leather" cut setting improve results.

5

DON'T MIRROR: Faux leather usually cuts face-up, not mirrored, so make sure the Mirror feature isn't toggled on.

6

PEEL THE MAT AWAY: Instead of peeling the faux leather off of the mat, flip the mat over and peel the mat away from the faux leather. This keeps your material smooth and crease-free.

PRINTABLE MATERIALS TIPS AND TRICKS

Printable materials open up a whole new world of full-color crafting, but they also add a few extra steps that can trip you up. Here's how to avoid common mistakes so your Print Then Cut projects come out crisp, accurate, and frustration-free.

1

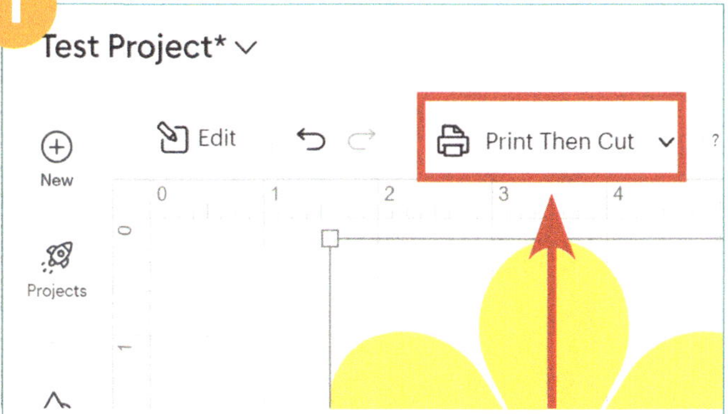

USE PRINT THEN CUT: Printable materials won't work right with the Operation set to Basic Cut, so make sure you have your design's Operation set to Print Then Cut on the Design Space Canvas.

2

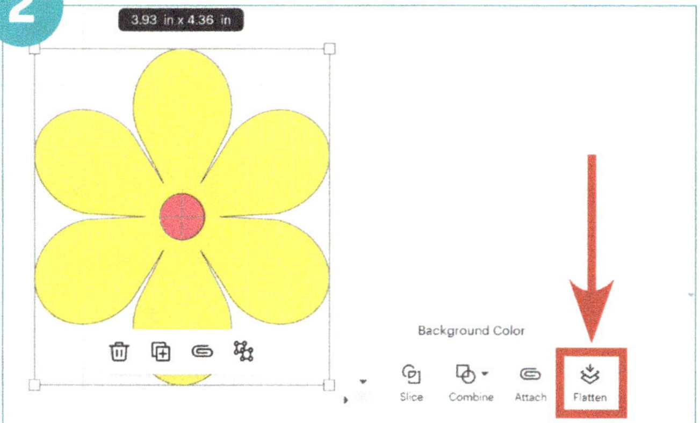

FLATTEN BEFORE PRINTING: On the Design Space Canvas, select your entire design and click the "Flatten" button. This makes your design all one piece and ensures everything prints and cuts in the right places.

3

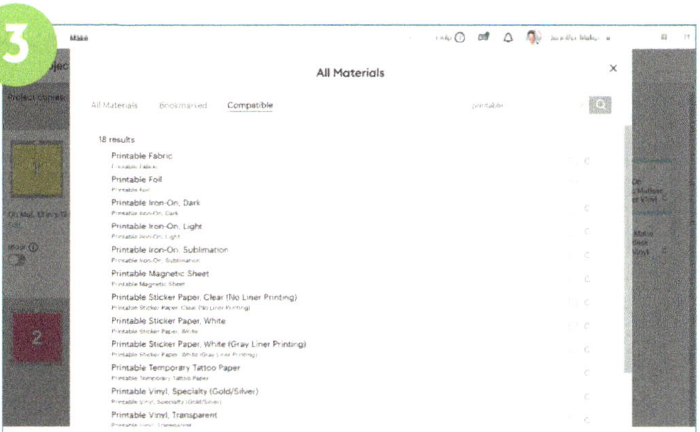

CHOOSE THE RIGHT CUT SETTING: This affects cut depth and accuracy, so choose the right printable material setting. There are quite a few listed in Design Space, like dark, light, and sublimation subtypes.

4

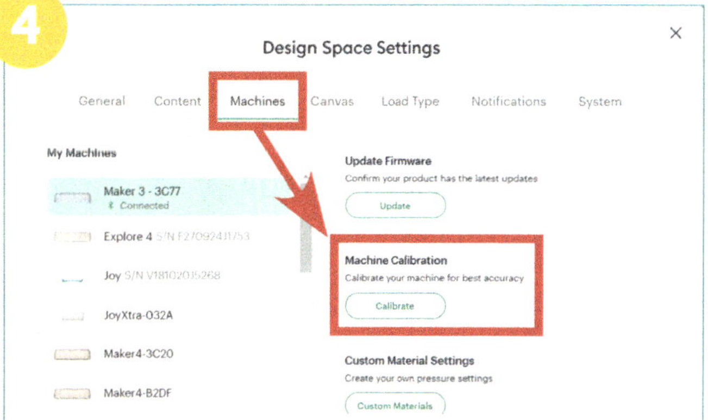

CALIBRATE IF CUTS ARE OFF: Design Space may prompt you to calibrate Print Then Cut settings. You can also calibrate if your design isn't cutting out correctly by clicking on your name, then "Settings," then "Machines," then "Calibrate."

FORGETTING STABILIZER FOR FABRIC

Stabilizer can feel optional until your fabric stretches or frays. This cheat sheet explains when stabilizer is essential and how to use it correctly. You don't need to use stabilizer with Maker series machines.

1

CUT A PIECE OF STABILIZER: Cut a piece of stabilizer the same size (or slightly smaller) as your material. Place the shiny adhesive side of the stabilizer on the wrong side of your fabric.

2

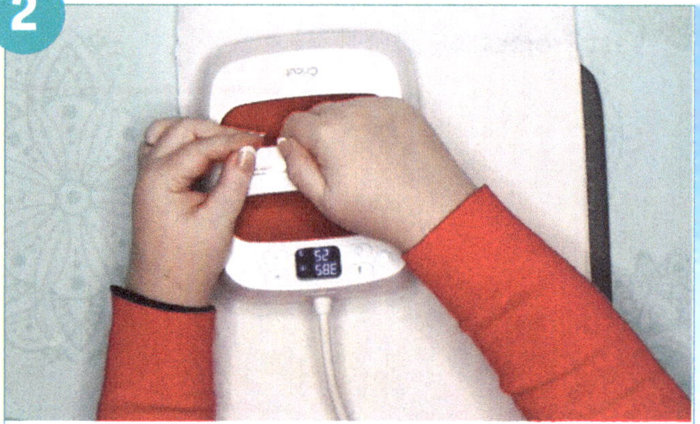

APPLY STABILIZER SMOOTHLY AND EVENLY: Wrinkles or bubbles in the stabilizer can distort the cut path. Adhere the stabilizer to the fabric with a household iron or heat press on a protected surface.

3

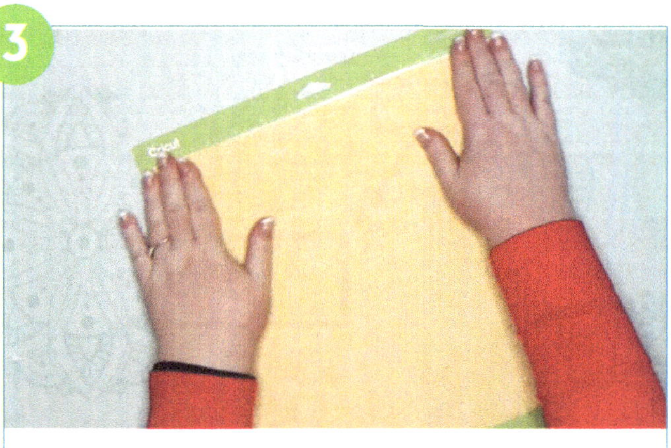

PUT STABILIZER FACE DOWN ON MAT: The stabilizer supports the fibers during cutting, but it can tear if it's face up on the mat. Make sure the fabric side is what you see on your mat.

4

USE A MAKER MACHINE: Because the Maker, Maker 3, and Maker 4 machines can use the Rotary Wheel tool, you don't need to attach stabilizer to your fabric. Just put your fabric straight onto the mat!

BASSWOOD OR VENEER CHIPPING OR CRACKING

Wood projects need patience and proper prep. These steps will help prevent cracking and chipping so your basswood cuts cleanly and safely on your Explore and Maker machines.

1

CHECK THE GRAIN DIRECTION BEFORE PLACING THE WOOD VENEER: Cutting against the grain increases the risk of cracking. Place the wood veneer so that the grain is running vertically.

2

USE A BRAYER: Use a brayer to firmly adhere the wood piece to the purple StrongGrip mat. This helps create a strong foundation before applying painter's tape.

3

SECURE ALL EDGES FIRMLY TO THE MAT: Movement during cutting increases cracking risk. Tape generously around the perimeter using painter's tape. Don't put tape where the Cricut will cut or where the gray rollers will interact with the mat.

4

PEEL THE MAT AWAY FROM THE WOOD: Do this rather than trying to peel the cut wood pieces up off of the mat, which is likely to cause cracks, splinters, and breaks. Flip the mat over and peel it away from the wood pieces instead.

PRINT THEN CUT SURVIVAL

- Print Then Cut Feature Missing
- My Print Then Cut is the Wrong Paper Size
- Print Then Cut Isn't Printing Correctly
- My Print Then Cut Calibration Won't Save
- My Print Then Cut Cuts Are Off
- When Should I Recalibrate Print Then Cut?
- Why Isn't My Print Then Cut Scanning?
- Using Glossy Paper with Print Then Cut
- Tape Hacks for Print Then Cut
- Scaling Issues Between Printer and Design Space
- Bleed Turned On or Off
- Wrong Paper Size Selected
- Print Then Cut Warning Messages

PRINT THEN CUT FEATURE MISSING

If you don't see Print Then Cut, don't worry. It's usually a setup issue, not a software problem. Let's look at the most common reasons this feature seems to disappear.

1

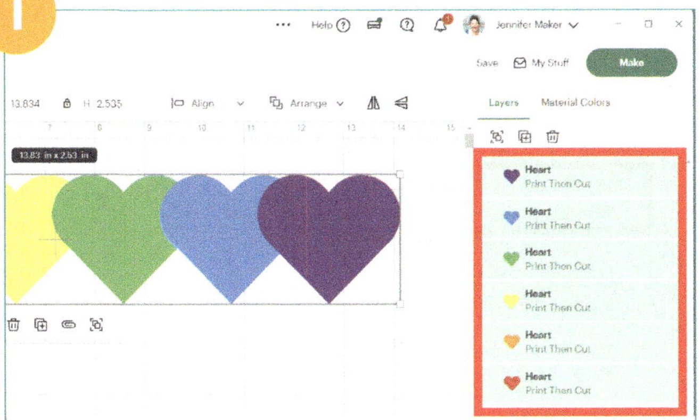

CONFIRM YOUR IMAGE TYPE: Print Then Cut only works with images that are set to Print Then Cut, not Basic Cut. Select your image and check the Operation menu.

2

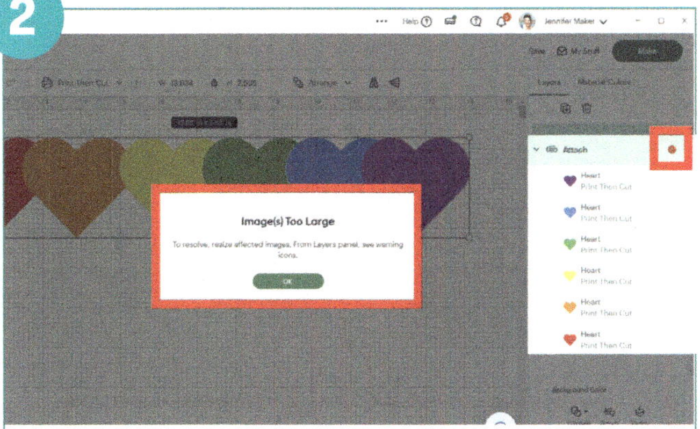

CHECK THE DESIGN SIZE: If your design is too large, Print Then Cut may not be available. You'll see a warning in the Layers Panel and get an error message when you click "Make." Resize your design to fit within Print Then Cut limits.

3

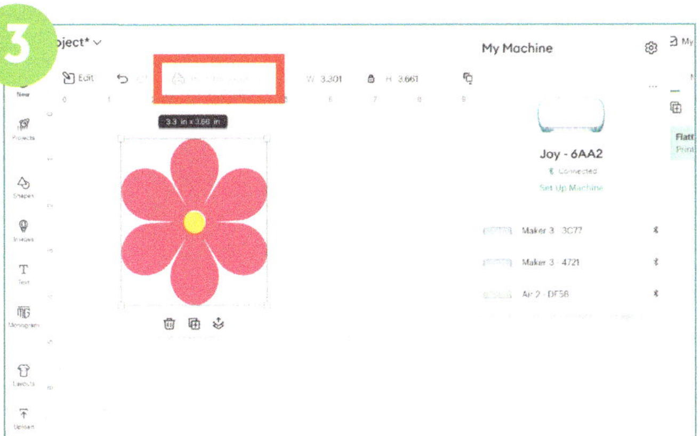

VERIFY YOUR MACHINE SELECTION: Make sure a Cricut machine that supports Print Then Cut is selected. Some features won't appear until a compatible machine is chosen. The Cricut Joy does not support Print Then Cut.

4

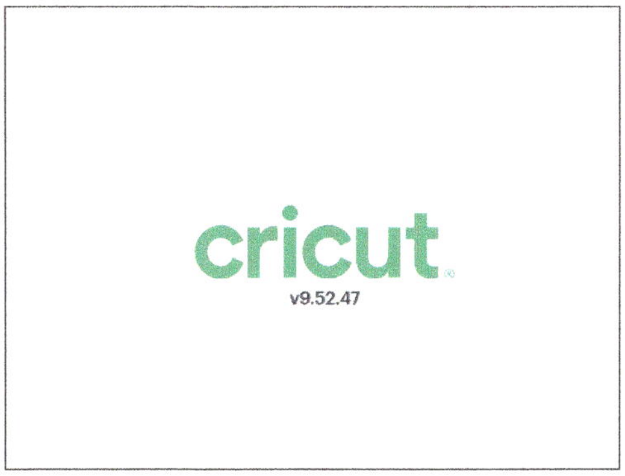

RESTART DESIGN SPACE: Close Design Space completely and reopen it. Missing features often reappear after a quick restart.

MY PRINT THEN CUT IS THE WRONG PAPER SIZE

If your Print Then Cut preview doesn't match your paper or your design prints too big or too small it's almost always a paper size or scaling issue.

1

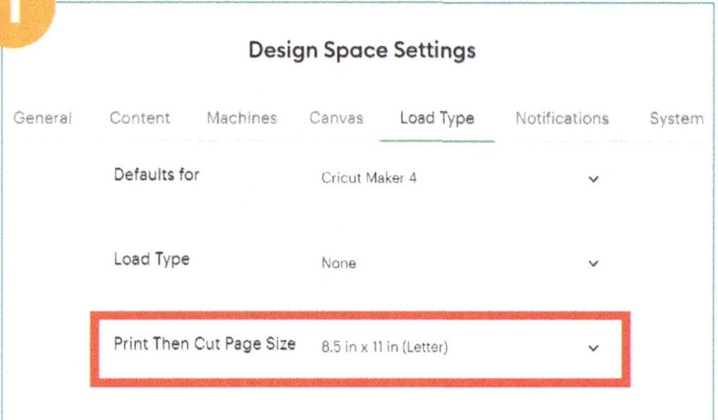

SET THE CORRECT PAPER SIZE IN DESIGN SPACE: Before designing, confirm the paper size selected in Design Space matches the paper you're using by clicking your name, then "Settings," then "Load Type."

2

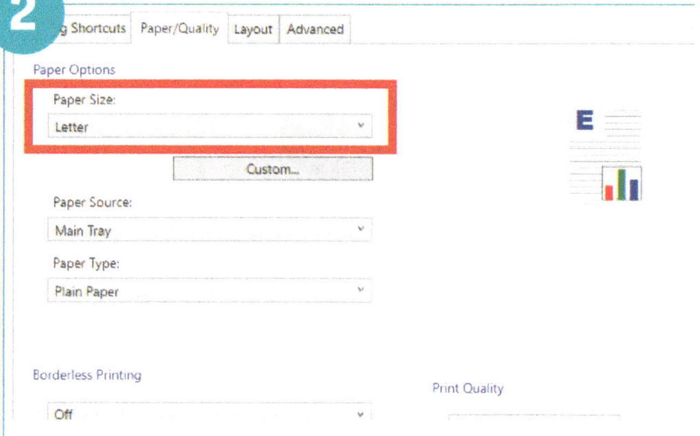

MATCH THE PRINTER PAPER SETTINGS: Once you've started the "Make" process, when the printer dialog opens, double-check the paper size there, too. Printer settings can override Design Space if they don't match.

3

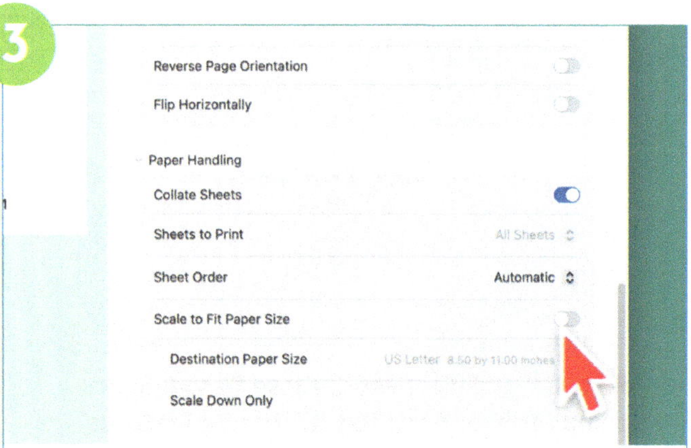

TURN OFF SCALING OPTIONS: Make sure options like Fit to Page, Scale to Fit, or Shrink to Printable Area are turned off. Print Then Cut must print at 100% for accurate cutting.

4

DO A TEST PRINT ON PLAIN PAPER: Before using specialty paper, print on plain paper first. This lets you confirm sizing and alignment without wasting materials.

PRINT THEN CUT ISN'T PRINTING CORRECTLY

Print errors can be frustrating, especially when everything looks right on the screen. Most printing issues come down to printer settings, not your design.

1

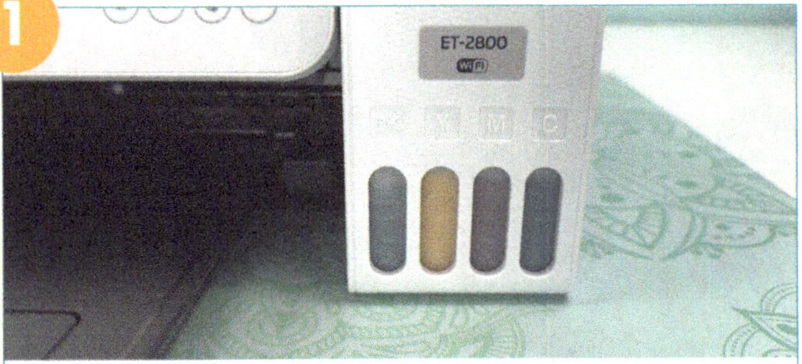

CHECK INK LEVELS: Low or uneven ink can affect sensor marks and cause cutting problems. Replace or refill ink if needed.

2

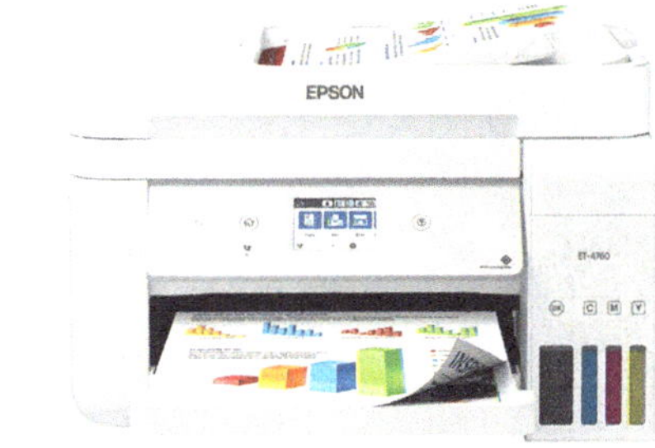

USE A SUPPORTED PRINTER: Print Then Cut works best with inkjet printers. Laser printers can cause issues with sensor marks and cutting accuracy.

3

USE GOOD LIGHTING WHILE SCANNING: When it's time to cut, make sure the Cricut has good lighting and the paper is flat on the mat so it can read the sensor marks clearly.

4

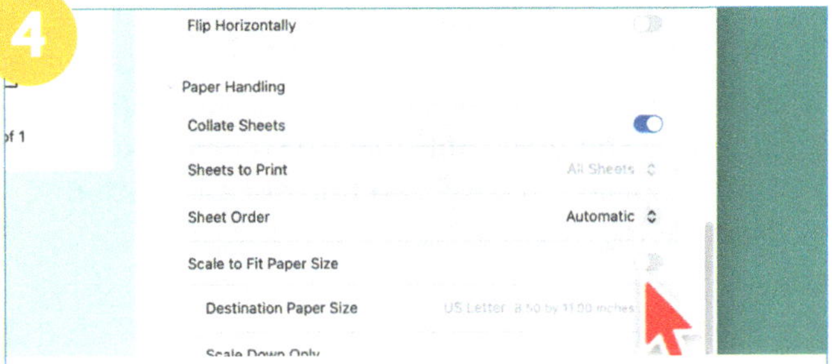

PRINT SETTINGS: Make sure your printer is set to print at 100% or Actual Size. Scaling can throw off the cut. Use the highest quality print setting.

5

REPRINT IF NEEDED: If the print looks smudged, faded, or uneven, reprint before cutting. Clean prints lead to clean cuts.

6

RESTART AND RETRY: If errors continue, restart your printer and Design Space, then try again with a fresh print.

MY PRINT THEN CUT CALIBRATION WON'T SAVE

If you finish calibration but it won't save – or you're asked to calibrate again next time – don't worry. This usually means something interrupted the process. Let's make sure your calibration actually sticks.

1

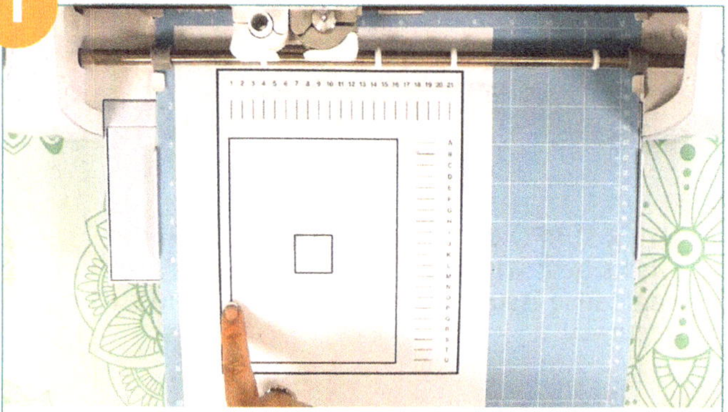

FINISH THE ENTIRE CALIBRATION PROCESS: Make sure you complete all calibration steps, including the final confirmation screen. Closing Design Space too early can prevent calibration from saving.

2

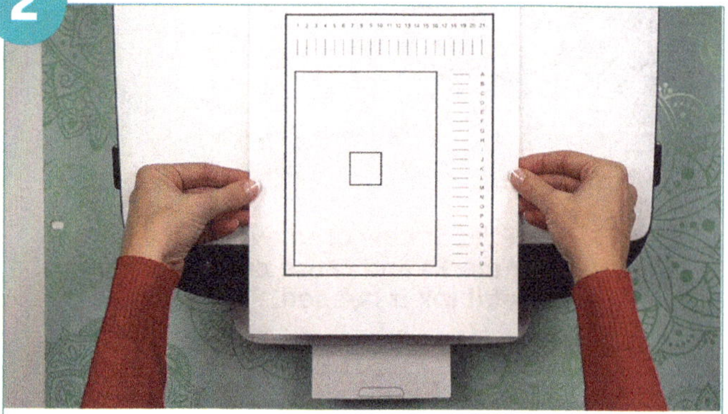

USE PLAIN WHITE PAPER: Calibration works best on plain white printer paper. Specialty papers or textured cardstock can interfere with accurate scanning.

3

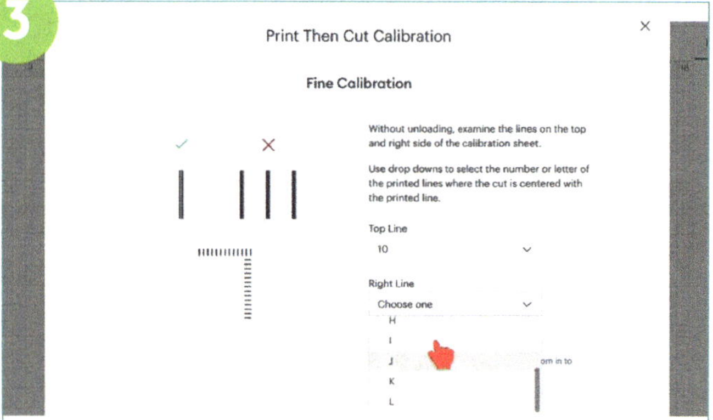

DON'T INTERRUPT THE PROCESS: Don't move the mat, close Design Space, or let your device go to sleep. Interruptions, including internet connectivity issues, can cancel the save.

4

RESTART AND TEST: After calibration finishes, restart Design Space and run a small Print Then Cut test to confirm the calibration was saved.

MY PRINT THEN CUT CUTS ARE OFF

It can be frustrating when your Print Then Cut cuts aren't actually cutting along the lines of your design. These steps will help you fix that.

1

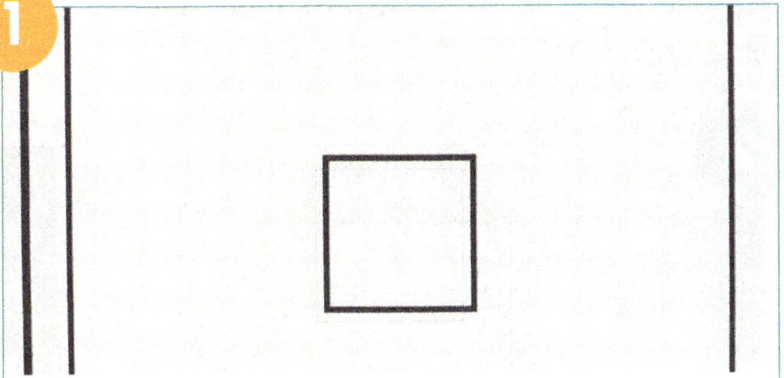

CHECK CALIBRATION FIRST: If your cuts are slicing into your image, or leaving too much white space, your Cricut is having trouble reading or aligning the print.

2

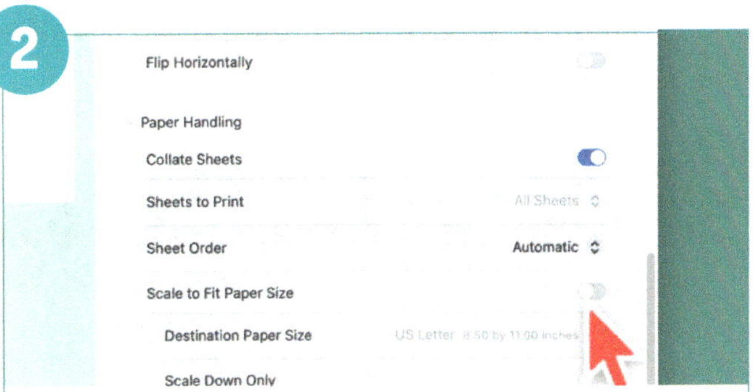

CONFIRM YOU PRINTED AT 100%: Make sure your printer settings were set to Actual Size or 100%. Any scaling will throw off the cut.

3

INSPECT THE SENSOR MARKS: Look closely at the black sensor marks. They should be crisp, dark, and not smudged or faded.

4

IMPROVE LIGHTING: Good lighting helps your Cricut read the sensor marks. Avoid harsh shadows, glare, or very dim lighting.

5

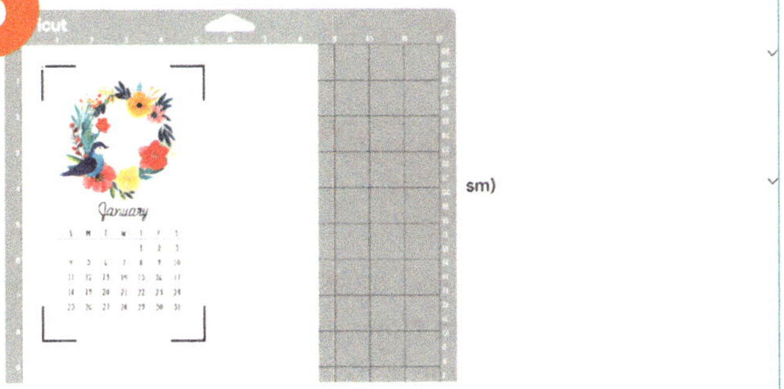

PLACE THE PAGE ON THE MAT CORRECTLY: Place the printed page on the mat as shown on the "Preview" screen to ensure proper cutting.

6

REPRINT IF NEEDED: If the print looks uneven, faded, or damaged, reprint before cutting. Clean prints lead to accurate cuts.

WHEN SHOULD I RECALIBRATE PRINT THEN CUT?

Calibration is helpful--but it's not something you need to do all the time. Recalibrating too often can actually create more problems. Here's how to know when it's truly needed.

1

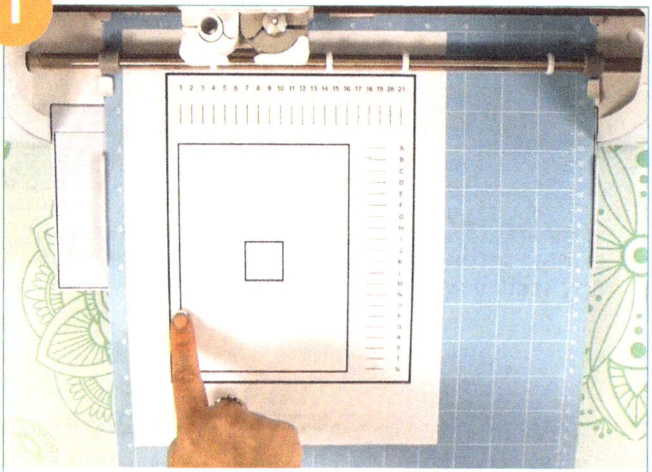

WHEN CUTS ARE OFF: If your Print Then Cut cuts are consistently misaligned, recalibration is the right first step.

2

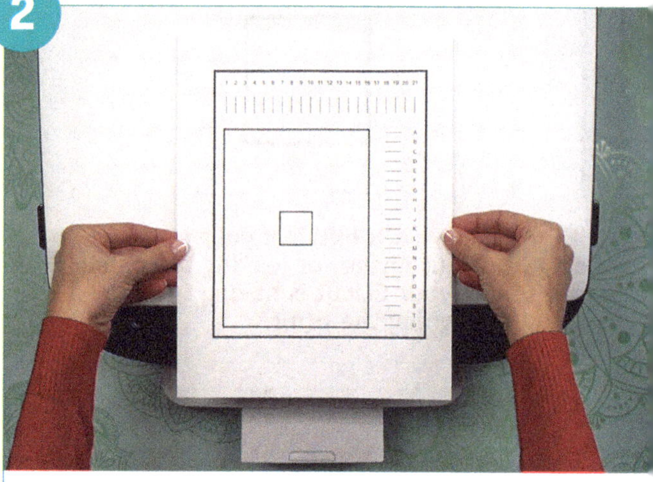

AFTER SOFTWARE OR MACHINE CHANGES: Recalibrate after major Design Space updates, firmware updates, or switching to a new device.

3

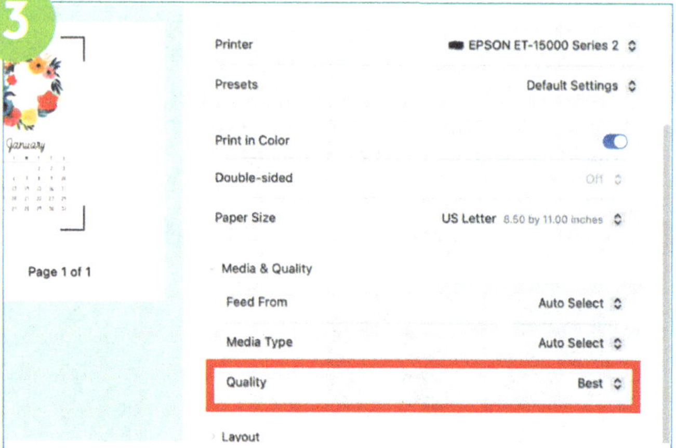

DON'T RECALIBRATE FOR PRINT ISSUES: If the problem is poor print quality, wrong paper size, or faded ink, calibration won't fix it. Address printing first.

4

AVOID RECALIBRATING REPEATEDLY: If calibration didn't help the first time, repeating it over and over usually won't fix the issue. Look for lighting, paper, or printer settings instead.

WHY ISN'T MY PRINT THEN CUT SCANNING?

If your Cricut is struggling to read the sensor marks, the issue is often lighting -- not your machine. A few simple adjustments can make scanning quick and reliable.

1

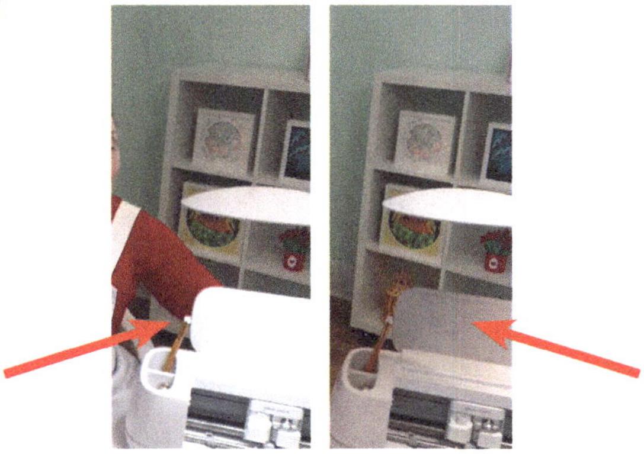

USE EVEN LIGHTING: Make sure your workspace is well lit. Overhead lighting works best so the sensor marks are evenly illuminated. Sometimes your lights can be too bright, so try turning them off and see if that helps.

2

AVOID SHADOWS AND GLARE: Remove strong directional lights that cast shadows across the page. Avoid shiny light sources that create glare on the paper.

3

USE MATTE PAPER: Use matte paper for your Print Then Cut designs. If you need to use glossy paper, you can print the design on matte paper, cut the design out but leave the sensor marks and tape it to the glossy paper.

4

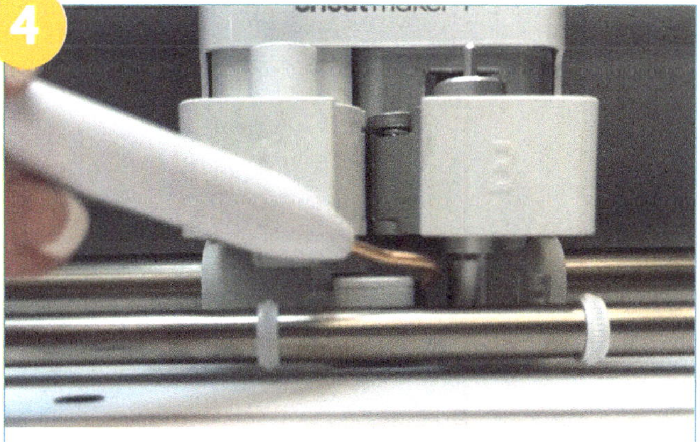

CLEAN THE SENSOR: If scanning fails, use a small brush to clean any paper debris off the scanner light. The sensor is located in this black box indicated here by the weeding tool.

USING GLOSSY PAPER WITH PRINT THEN CUT

Glossy and specialty papers can be tricky because they reflect light, making it harder for the Cricut to read sensor marks. These tips help reduce glare and improve scan success.

1

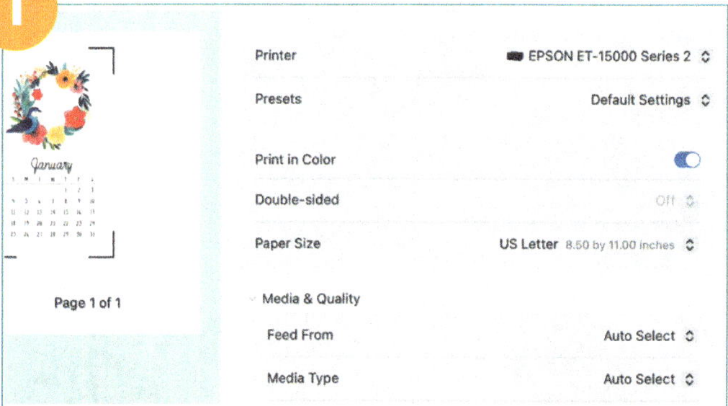

CHOOSE MATTE SETTINGS WHEN POSSIBLE: If your printer offers a matte or plain paper setting, use it -- even when printing on glossy paper. This often reduces shine. Your printer may have Auto Select, which is typically the plain paper setting.

2

LET THE INK DRY COMPLETELY: Allow printed pages to dry fully before cutting. Wet ink reflects more light and can interfere with scanning.

3

REDUCE GLARE: Turn off bright overhead lights or move the machine slightly to minimize reflections on the paper.

4

TRY A TAPE FRAME: If scanning still fails, lightly frame the sensor marks with matte tape -- without covering them -- to reduce glare.

TAPE HACKS FOR PRINT THEN CUT

Tape can be a helpful last-resort fix when Print Then Cut won't scan -- but it needs to be used correctly. These steps show when tape helps and how to use it without creating new problems.

1

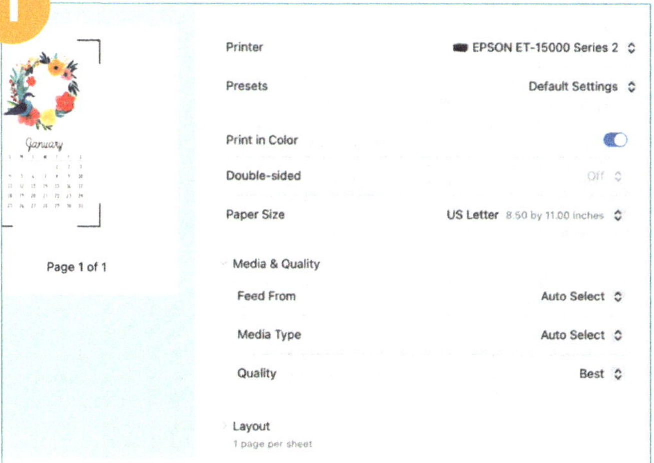

USE TAPE ONLY AFTER OTHER FIXES FAIL: Try adjusting lighting and paper settings first. Tape should be used only if scanning still fails.

2

CHOOSE MATTE NOT GLOSSY TAPE: Use matte scotch tape. Avoid shiny or clear tape, which can reflect light and confuse the scanner.

3

USE PLAIN PAPER SENSOR MARKS: Print the same image on a plain sheet of paper, cut out the image leaving the sensor marks, and tape the sensor marks on the glossy page making sure both sets of sensor marks line up.

4

KEEP THE TAPE FLAT AND SMOOTH: Press the tape down firmly so there are no wrinkles, bubbles, or lifted edges. Uneven tape can create shadows that interfere with scanning.

SCALING ISSUES BETWEEN PRINTER AND DESIGN SPACE

Print Then Cut problems often start with scaling mismatches. These steps will help you align Design Space, printer settings, and calibration for accurate cuts.

1

RESIZE DESIGNS ONLY ON THE CANVAS: Never resize a design during the printing process. These changes will cause misalignment and miscuts.

2

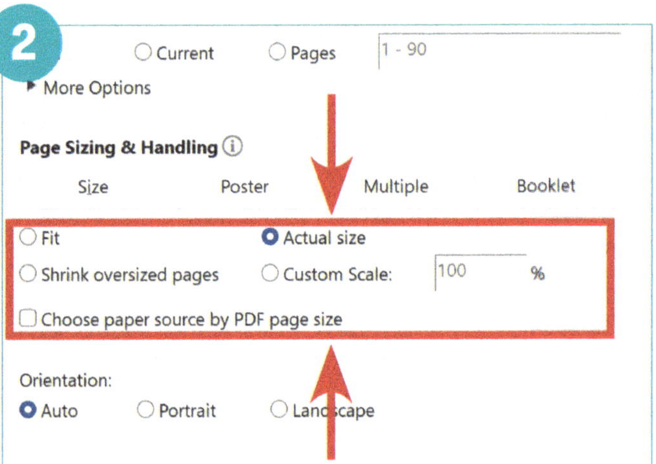

TURN OFF SCALING IN PRINTER SETTINGS: Disable "Fit to Page" or "Scale to Fit." These settings alter size accuracy. Use "Actual Size" or "100%."

3

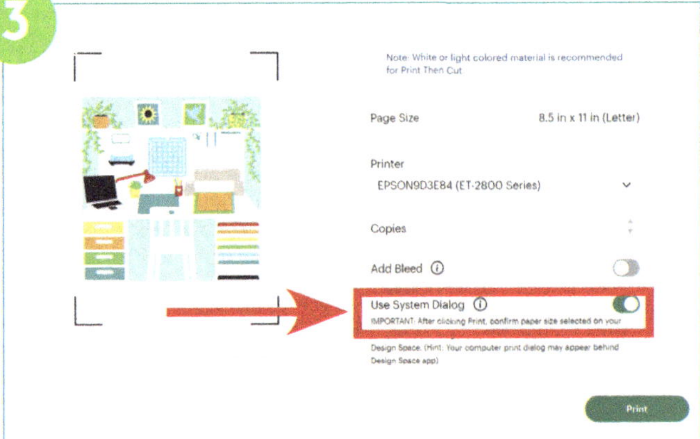

USE THE SYSTEM DIALOG WHEN PRINTING: This gives full access to printer controls. Cricut's default dialog may hide scaling options.

4

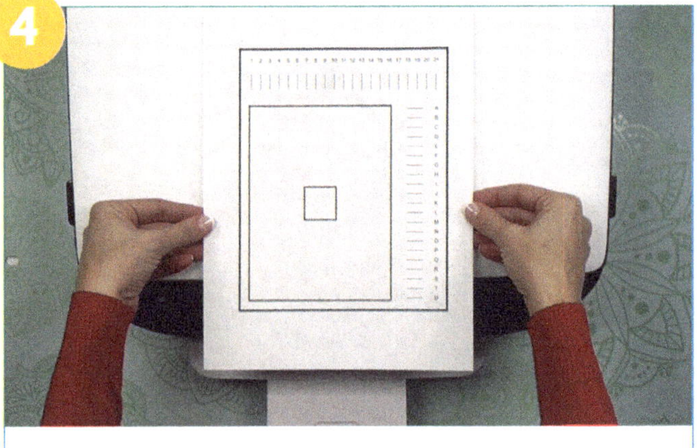

PRINT AND CUT A CALIBRATION SHEET: Calibration aligns your machine to your printer to improve accuracy. Find it by clicking your name, "Settings," "Machines," and "Machine Calibration."

BLEED TURNED ON OR OFF

Bleed can be your best friend, or totally unnecessary, depending on your design. This guide helps you choose the right setting every time.

1

WITH BLEED WITHOUT BLEED

UNDERSTAND WHAT BLEED ACTUALLY DOES: Bleed extends ink slightly beyond the cut line. This prevents white edges, but can cause unwanted color as well. Use the right setting for your design.

2

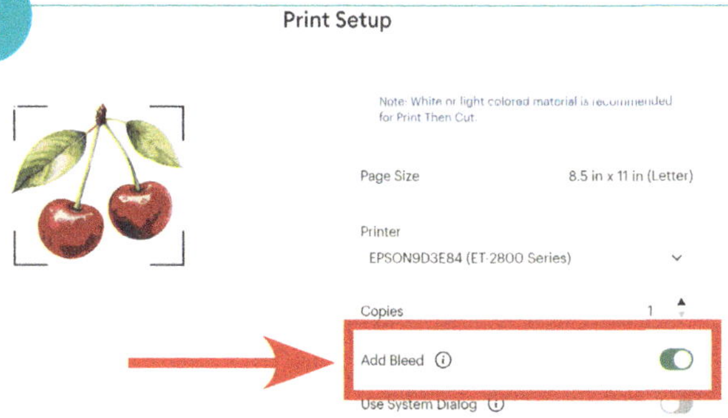

TURN BLEED ON FOR FULL-COLOR IMAGES: Photos and colorful designs benefit from bleed. It hides small cut inaccuracies.

3

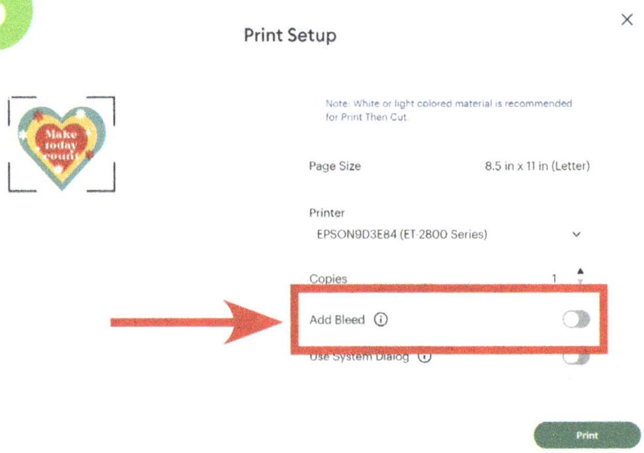

TURN BLEED OFF FOR PRECISE DESIGNS: Logos or white-border stickers often look cleaner without bleed. Precision matters here.

4

ALWAYS PREVIEW BEFORE PRINTING: The preview shows exactly how bleed will affect the design. Never skip this step.

WRONG PAPER SIZE SELECTED

Paper size mismatches are a sneaky cause of Print Then Cut failures. This cheat sheet shows how to keep Design Space and your printer perfectly synced.

1

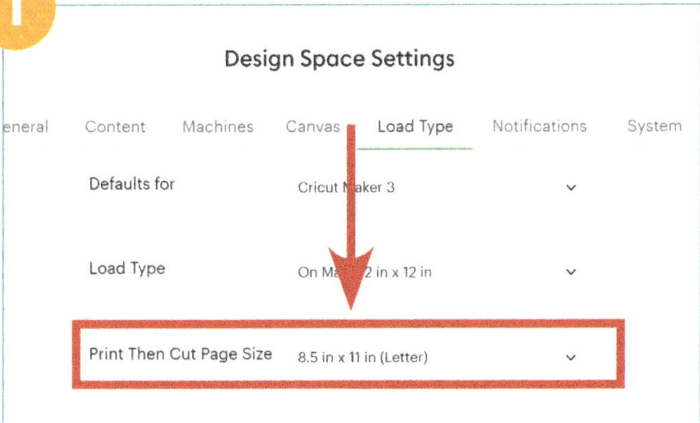

CHECK THE PAPER SIZE SETTING IN DESIGN SPACE: Paper sizes are not interchangeable. Check the default Print Then Cut paper size by clicking on your name, then "Settings," then "Load Type."

2

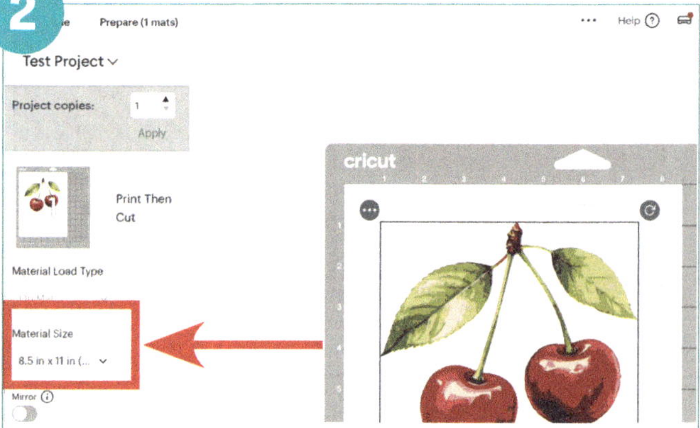

CONFIRM THE PAPER SIZE ON THE PREVIEW SCREEN: Make sure that the paper size under "Material Size" on the Mat Preview screen matches the paper size you intend to print your design on.

3

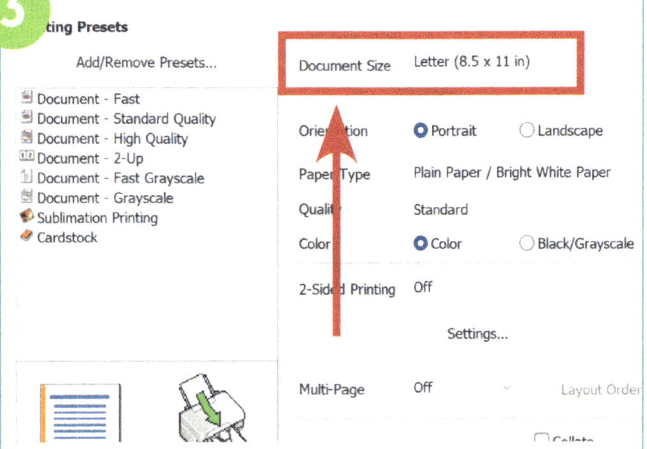

MATCH THE PAPER SIZE IN PRINTER SETTINGS: Both Design Space and the printer must agree. One mismatch breaks alignment.

4

REPRINT IF ANY SETTING CHANGES: Never reuse a print after changing settings. Always start fresh by printing a new copy of your design.

PRINT THEN CUT WARNING MESSAGES

Those warning pop-ups are trying to help, not annoy you. This guide explains what they mean and how to fix the issue before cutting.

1

CONFIRM THAT YOUR MACHINE SUPPORTS PRINT THEN CUT: The original Cricut Joy, like the one pictured here, cannot perform the Print Then Cut operation.

2

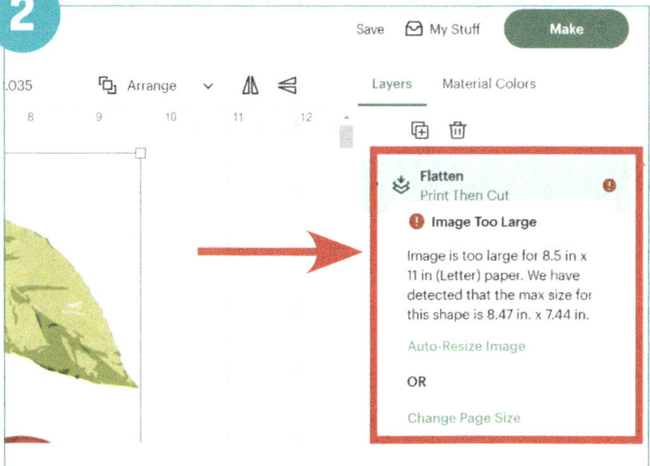

READ THE WARNING CAREFULLY INSTEAD OF DISMISSING IT: Warnings usually explain the exact issue. Skipping them causes repeat problems.

3

Image Too Large

Image is too large for 8.5 in x 14 in (Legal) paper. We have detected that the max size for this shape is 8.47 in. x 7.44 in.

Auto-Resize Image

OR

Change Page Size

CHECK THE MAXIMUM PRINT THEN CUT SIZE: Design Space enforces strict size limits. Oversized designs trigger warnings.

4

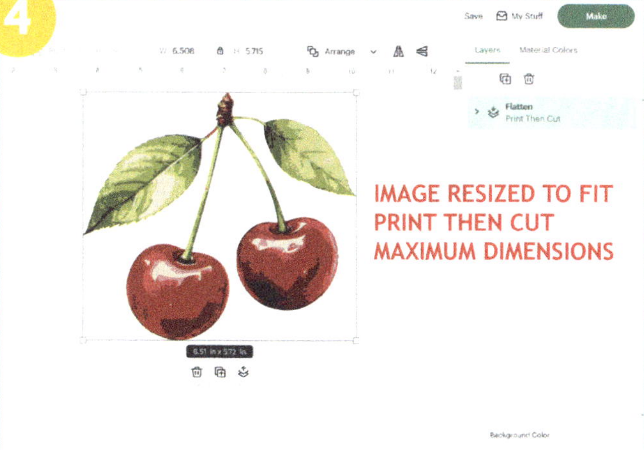

RESOLVE WARNINGS BEFORE PROCEEDING: Repeated warnings indicate unresolved setup problems. Fix them before cutting.

MATS, BLADES, AND TOOLS

- Cricut Mat is Not Sticky
- Too Sticky vs. Not Sticky Enough
- Choosing the Right Mat
- Cricut Blades and Uses
- When to Replace Blades

CRICUT MAT IS NOT STICKY

If your material won't stay put on your Cricut mat, you're not alone. It happens to everyone. Here's why your mat isn't gripping and what to try to get back on track.

1

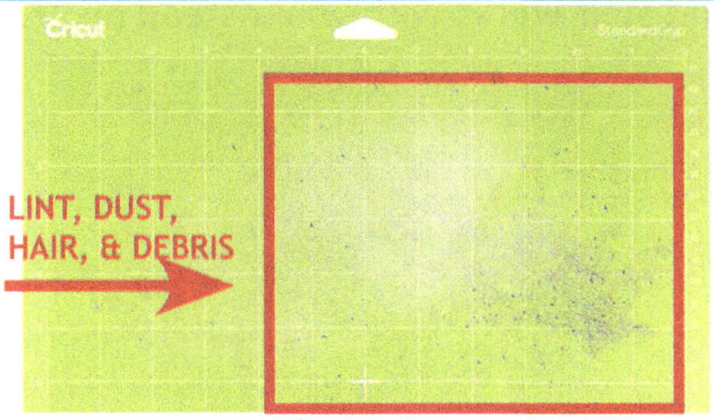

CHECK FOR SURFACE DEBRIS: Lint, paper dust, glitter, and pet hair are the #1 reason mats stop sticking. Even a mat that looks clean may not be. Clean it with a scraper tool first.

2

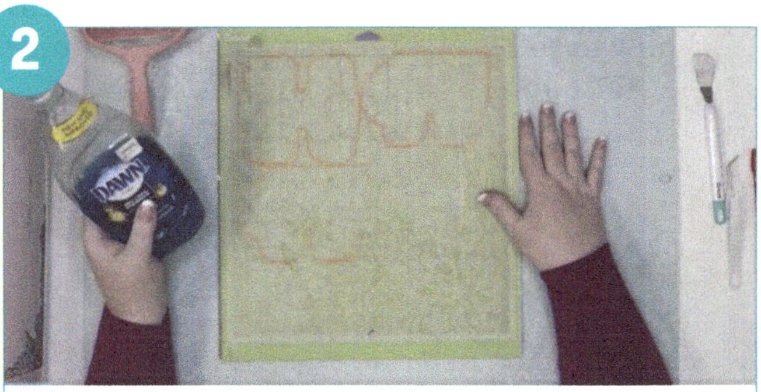

GENTLY CLEAN THE MAT: Use an alcohol-free baby wipe or warm water and a drop of mild dish soap. Gently scrub with your fingers or a soft brush, rinse well, and air dry completely.

3

LET THE STICKINESS REACTIVATE: After drying, the adhesive often becomes tacky again. This works best if the mat isn't too old. Wait 30-60 minutes after washing a mat to allow it to become sticky.

4

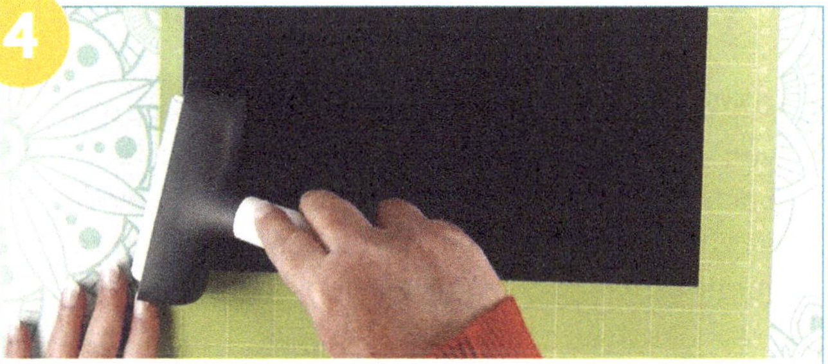

ADJUST HOW YOU LOAD MATERIALS: Burnish your material down firmly with a scraper or brayer, especially near edges and corners.

5

USE TEMPORARY HELP IF NEEDED: Painter's tape around the edges (not over the design) can help stabilize lightweight or curling materials.

6

KNOW WHEN IT'S TIME TO REPLACE: If the mat still won't hold after cleaning, it's likely reached the end of its life, and that's okay!

TOO STICKY VS NOT STICKY ENOUGH

A Cricut mat that's too sticky can be just as problematic as one that's worn out. Here's how to tell the difference and how to adjust your mat so it works with you instead of against you.

1

MATCH THE MAT TO THE MATERIAL: Make sure you're using the best mat for your material. Each mat has a different purpose, and they're easy to tell apart. For more about mats, go to jennifermaker.com/cricut-cutting-mats-sticky.

2

REDUCE STICKINESS IF IT'S TOO STRONG: Tap a clean cotton shirt, paper towel, or something similar onto the mat to gently reduce tack before placing your material.

3

INCREASE HOLD IF IT'S TOO WEAK: Burnish well using a brayer and tape edges using painter's tape, if needed. Make sure your mat is clean and fully dry.

4

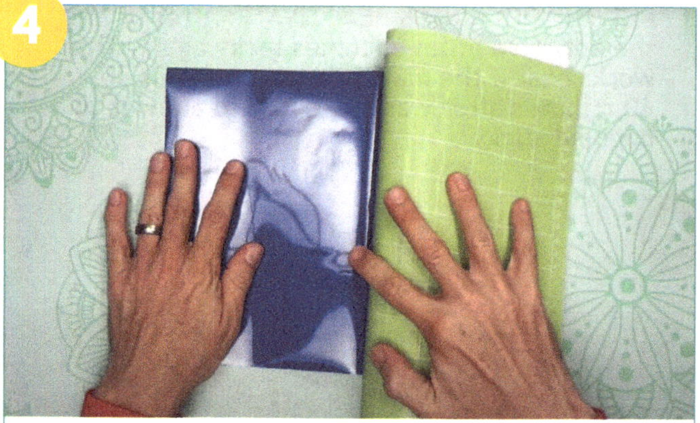

ADJUST REMOVAL TECHNIQUE: Flip the mat upside down and peel the mat away from the material rather than peeling the material away from the mat. This helps prevent curling and tearing.

CHOOSING THE RIGHT MAT

Cricut mats come in different grip strengths for a reason, and using the wrong one can cause tearing, slipping, or failed cuts. Each mat is color-coded and is for specific materials.

1

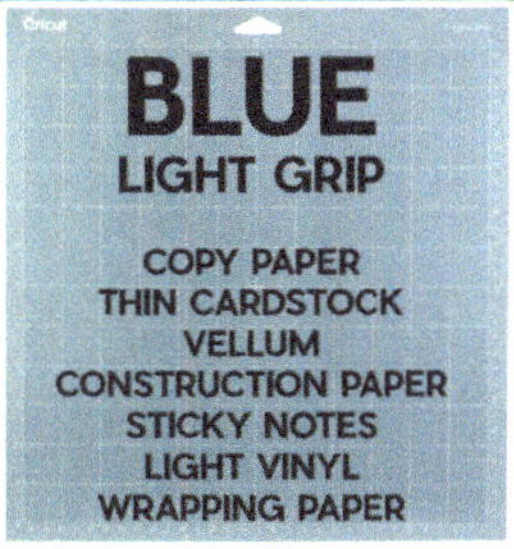

BLUE LIGHTGRIP MAT: This light-blue mat is perfect for delicate materials like printer paper, scrapbook paper, vellum, and light cardstock. It holds materials just enough to cut cleanly without tearing when you remove them.

2

GREEN STANDARDGRIP MAT: This is your everyday mat! It works beautifully for vinyl, iron-on, medium cardstock, and most common craft materials. If you're not sure which mat to grab, this one is usually the right choice.

3

PURPLE STRONGGRIP MAT: This purple mat has extra-strong adhesive to hold thick or heavy materials like wood veneer, leather, and chipboard in place. Always use a brayer and tape edges when needed. (Not available for Cricut Joy)

4

PINK FABRICGRIP MAT: Designed specifically for fabric, the gentle adhesive grips fabric fibers without damaging them, especially when paired with a rotary blade. Only use this mat for fabric. (Not available for Cricut Joy)

5

CARD MAT: These special mats are made just for cutting card fronts, including the special insert cards made by Cricut. On Explore & Maker series machines, move the star wheels to the center of the rail when using card mats.

6

MATCH MATERIAL, NOT JUST THICKNESS: It's not just about how thick something is - fragile materials can tear on overly sticky mats, while heavier materials may slide on lighter mats. Think about flexibility and surface texture, too.

CRICUT BLADES AND USES

With so many blade options, it's easy to wonder which one to use and when. From Fine-Point to Deep-Point to specialty blades, each has a specific job it does best.

1

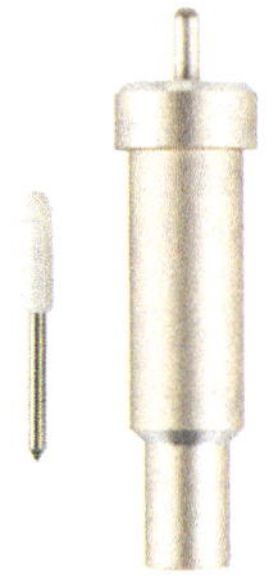

FINE-POINT BLADE: This is your go-to blade for vinyl, iron-on, cardstock, and most everyday projects. It's sharp, long-lasting, and ideal for crafters who cut often.

2

DEEP-POINT BLADE: Use this blade when materials are thicker or denser, like magnet sheets or thicker cardstock. It has a steeper angle to handle extra resistance.

3

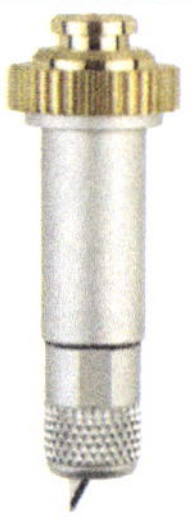

KNIFE BLADE: The knife blade is reserved for thick materials like basswood and leather. This blade cuts in multiple passes, so patience is key. Don't rush it, and always follow Cricut's material guidelines.

4

ROTARY BLADE: When paired with a FabricGrip mat, it rolls smoothly through the fibers of fabric instead of dragging and tearing them. This is only for use in the Maker series of Cricut machines.

5

ENGRAVING TIP: This specialty tip is used for engraving designs into materials like acrylic, metal, and coated surfaces. It doesn't cut, but instead etches for a permanent look. This is only for use in the Maker series of Cricut machines.

6

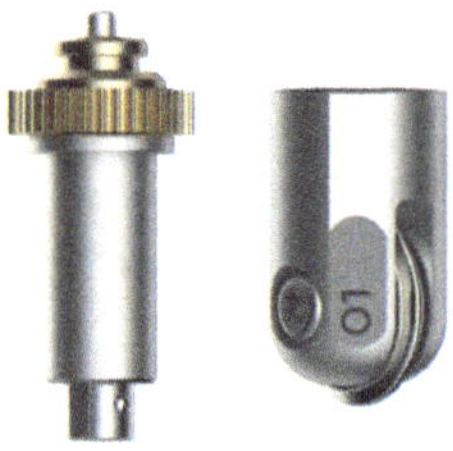

SCORING TIP: This tip is perfect for clean fold lines on cards, boxes, and 3D projects. Scoring before folding gives you crisp edges and polished results every time. This is only for use in the Maker series of Cricut machines.

WHEN TO REPLACE BLADES

Blades don't last forever, and a dull blade can cause more problems than you might expect. If you're seeing frayed edges, incomplete cuts, or needing extra pressure, it might be time for a new blade.

1

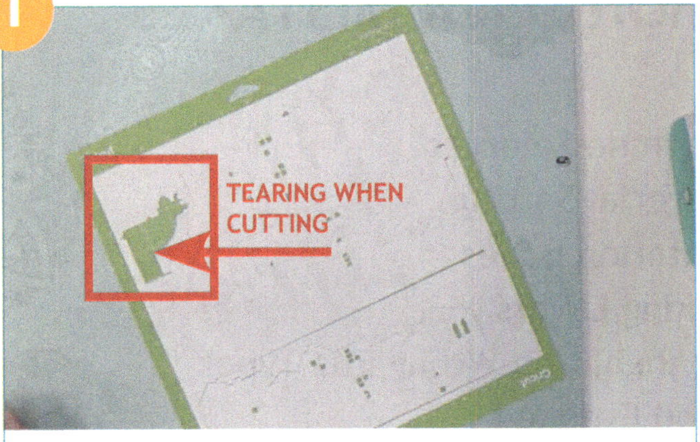

LOOK AT THE CUT QUALITY: If your cuts look jagged, torn, or incomplete, even with the correct settings, it's often a sign the blade is dull (or possibly dirty).

2

CLEAN THE BLADE FIRST: Try cleaning your blade by carefully using rubbing alcohol and a microfiber cloth. This should remove any stuck little pieces of material. Tiny scraps can prevent proper blade movement.

3

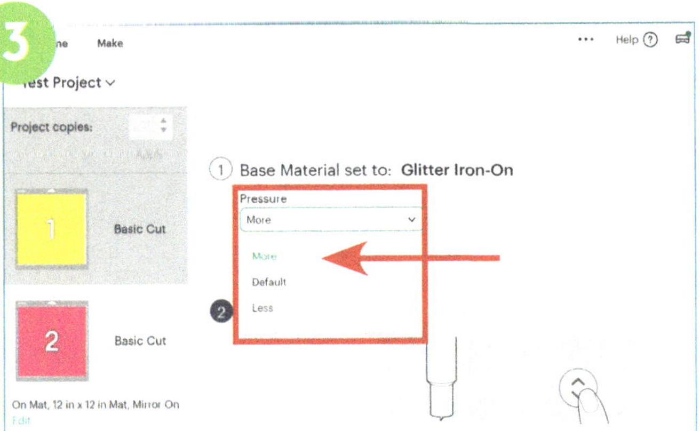

INCREASE PRESSURE SLIGHTLY: A small pressure increase can sometimes extend a blade's life. But if you're constantly adjusting pressure, that blade is probably on its way out. Either choose "More" Pressure or increase the pressure manually.

4

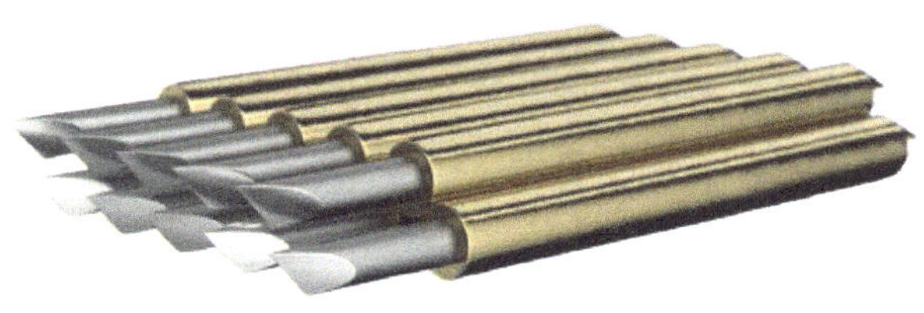

REPLACE THE BLADE: If issues continue across multiple materials and mats, don't fight it - it's time for a fresh blade. New blades make a huge difference! Avoid "Standard Blades," which are for older machines.

COMMON USER MISTAKES

- Wrong Machine Selected
- Wrong Material Setting
- Mat Orientation Issues
- Not Checking Layers
- Using the Right and Wrong File Types
- Mat Loaded Crooked
- Canvas Grid Turned Off or On
- Canvas Units Confusion
- Getting Charged for Elements with Access
- Which One Should I Use: Flatten, Attach, or Weld?
- Grouping When Attach is Needed
- Flattening When Attach is Needed
- Attaching When Flatten is Needed

WRONG MACHINE SELECTED

This is one of those sneaky mistakes that can stop a project before it even starts. If Design Space thinks you're using a different Cricut machine, your settings and cut options may not match what your machine can actually do.

1

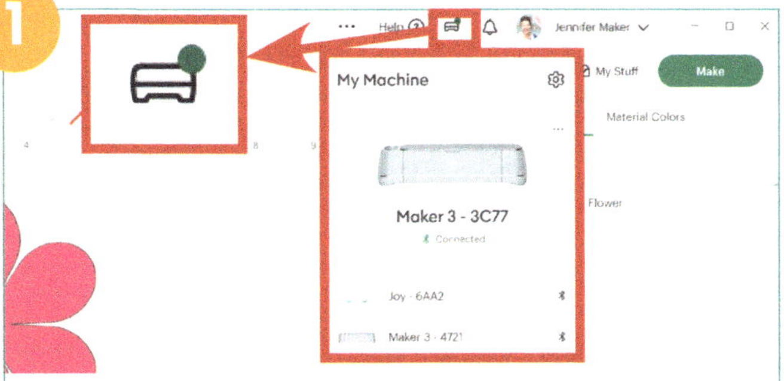

CONFIRM YOUR MACHINE: Click on the machine shown at the top of the Canvas window and select your machine. It does not automatically detect which machine is on.

2

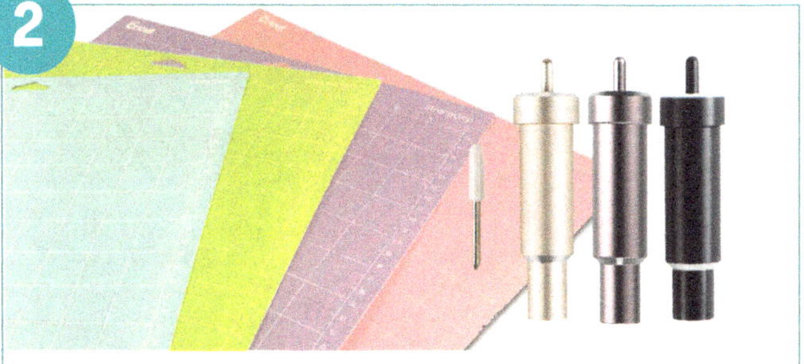

UNDERSTAND WHY THIS MATTERS: Each Cricut machine supports different tools, blades, materials, and mat sizes. If the wrong machine is selected, Design Space hides options you need or shows ones your machine can't use.

3

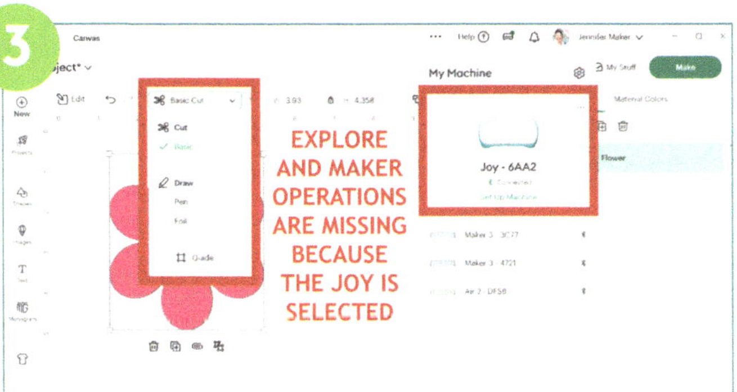

WATCH FOR MISSING FEATURES: If you don't see the Knife Blade, Rotary Blade, scoring options, or thicker material settings, that's usually a machine mismatch - not a software glitch.

4

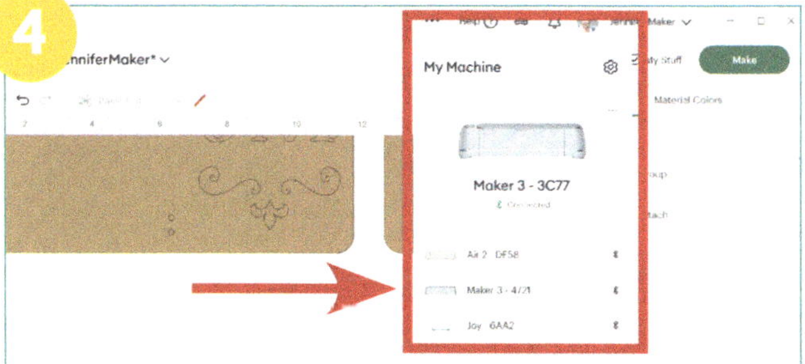

CHANGE MACHINE BEFORE EDITING PROJECT: Switching machines after resizing, attaching, or choosing materials can reset layouts and settings. Select the correct machine first.

5

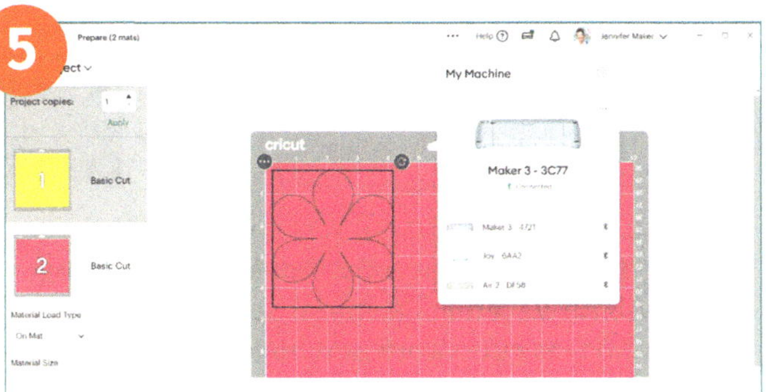

REOPEN THE MAKE SCREEN: If you have the wrong machine selected on the Make screens, select the right Cricut machine, exit and re-enter the Cut screen to refresh.

6

CREATE A FIRST-STEP HABIT: Make checking the machine your non-negotiable first step. It prevents a chain reaction of errors later.

WRONG MATERIAL SETTING

Choosing the wrong material setting can turn a great design into a cutting disaster. Too much pressure can slice through your mat, while too little leaves pieces uncut. Learn how to pick the right setting and know when to adjust it.

1

MATCH HOW THE MATERIAL BEHAVES: Shiny, textured, glittery, or flexible materials all cut differently, even if they're technically the same type of vinyl or cardstock.

2

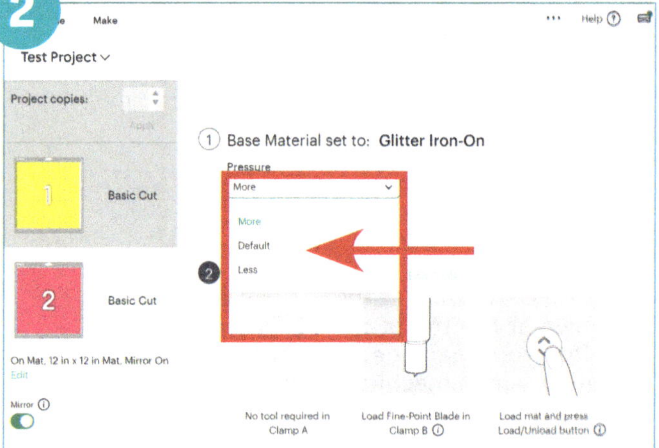

ADJUST PRESSURE GRADUALLY: Start with "Default" Pressure. Move to "More" only if needed. Jumping too high too fast can cause deep cuts, tearing, or mat damage.

3

USE TEST CUTS STRATEGICALLY: Do small test cuts in corners or unused areas of your material. This is especially important for specialty or expensive materials.

4

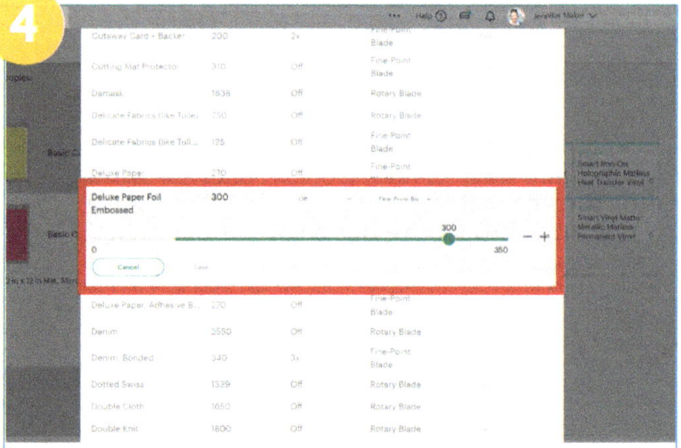

SAVE CUSTOM MATERIALS: When you find the perfect cut, save it as a Custom Material Setting (Browse All Materials, Material Settings, Edit). This removes guesswork and builds consistency.

MAT ORIENTATION ISSUES

The way you load your mat really does matter! Loading a mat upside down or flipped can cause misaligned cuts or designs cutting in the wrong spot.

1

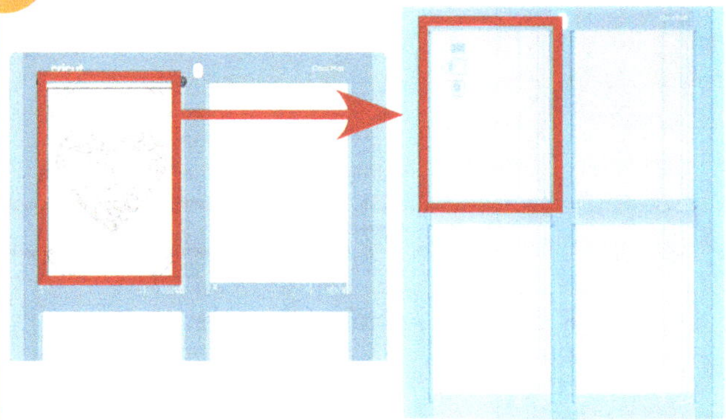

UNDERSTAND CUTTING ORIGIN: Cricut starts cutting from the top-left corner of the mat. That corner must match on screen and your physical mat. This doesn't matter for most 12x12 inch mats, but does for card and other sized mats.

2

WATCH FOR DESIGN ROTATION: Design Space may rotate designs to save material. This is helpful, but dangerous if direction, grain, or text orientation matters. If a part of your design got rotated, fix it on the Prepare screen.

3

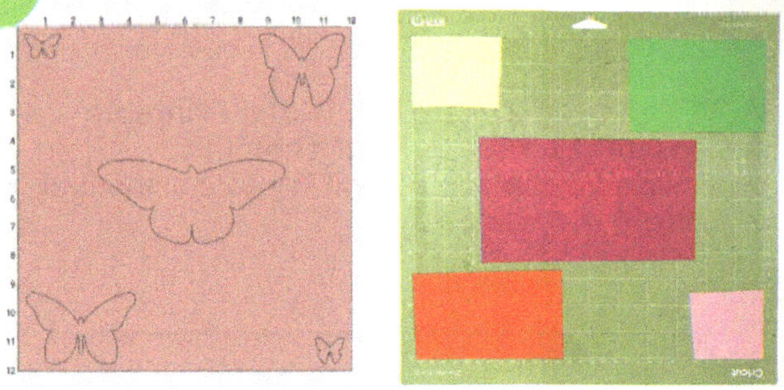

PLACE MATERIAL TO MATCH MATERIAL: If your design is positioned lower or rotated on screen, place your material the same way on the mat, not centered or just in the top left corner by habit. This is also important if you're cutting multiple colors of material on a single mat.

4

LOAD MAT CAREFULLY AND EVENLY: Always feed the mat straight into your Cricut machine using the raised guides so that both of the machine's rollers grab the mat at the same time. Crooked loading causes shifted or cut-off designs, bent or broken mats, and machine jams.

NOT CHECKING LAYERS

If layers aren't set correctly, your Cricut may cut when it should draw, or ignore parts of your design altogether. Here's what to check before clicking the "Make" button.

1

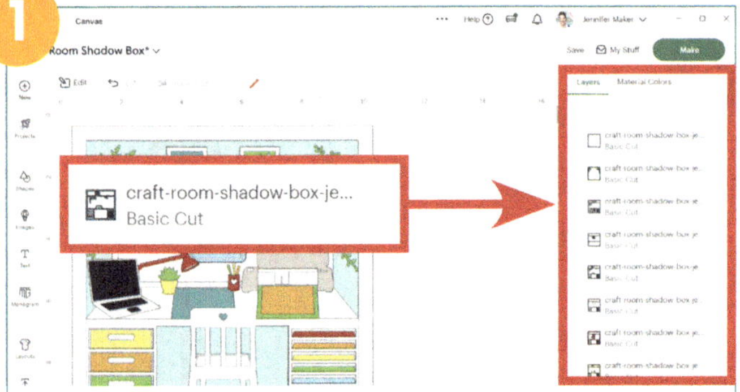

OPEN THE LAYERS PANEL: Even if the design looks fine on the canvas, hidden issues often live in the Layers panel, so always check.

2

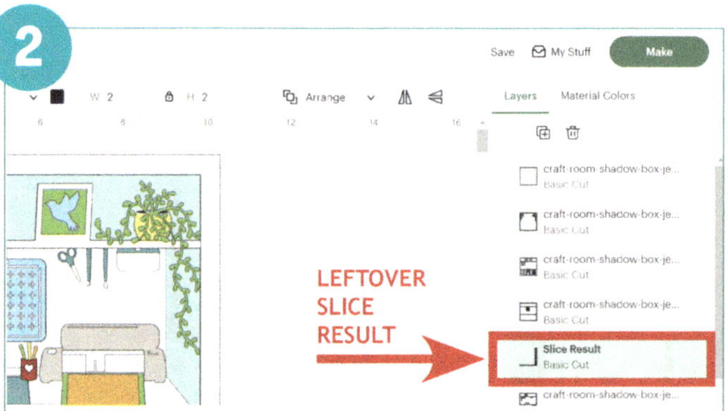

LOOK FOR EXTRAS: Accidental copies, leftover shapes from Slicing, or invisible layers can cause surprise cuts.

3

CONFIRM OPERATION TYPES: Each layer should be intentionally set to cut, score, pen, engrave, foil, deboss, or Print Then Cut. One wrong setting affects the entire project.

4

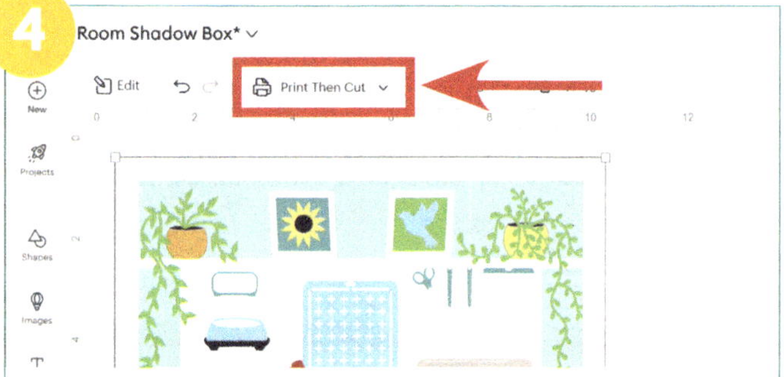

VERIFY PRINT THEN CUT DESIGNS: Printable designs must be set to Print Then Cut, otherwise your machine will try to cut instead of print.

5

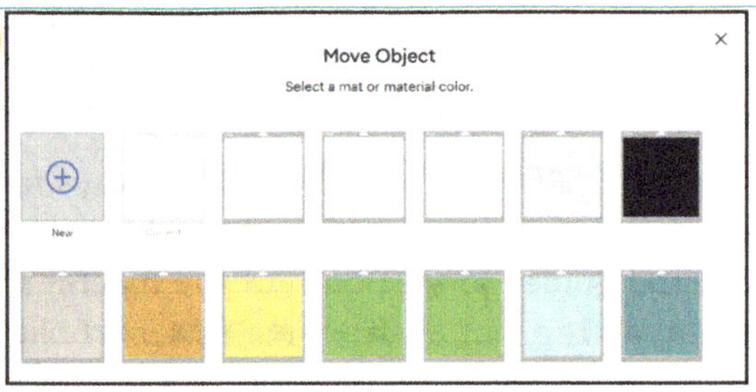

USE COLOR CODING INTENTIONALLY: Different colors mean separate mats. If a project splits, color is often the cause. Make sure you don't accidentally have similar shades of the same color when you actually only want one shade.

6

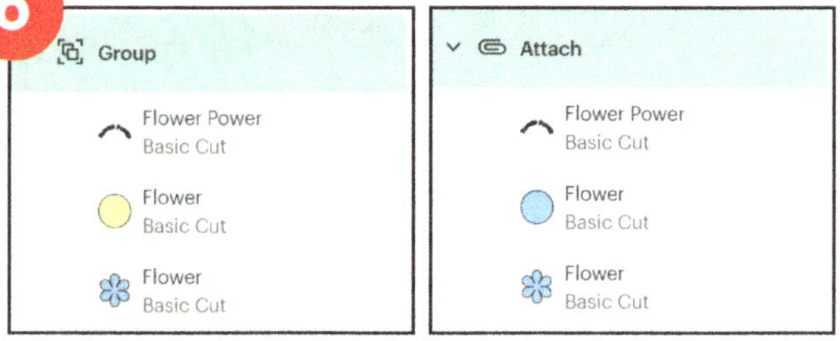

EDITING TOOLS AREN'T EQUAL CUTTING TOOLS: Group is for organizing elements on the Canvas and doesn't have any effect on cutting. Attach is for cutting accuracy and does determine which elements stay together when cutting.

USING THE RIGHT AND WRONG FILE TYPES

Not all file types work the same in Cricut Design Space, and choosing the wrong one can cause extra steps or major frustration. Learn which types to use and which ones to avoid.

1

UNDERSTAND IMAGE FILE TYPES: PNG and JPG files are images, not cut paths, and require manual cleanup. They often load as flat Print Then Cut images or single-layer cuts.

2

CHOOSE SVG FILES WHENEVER POSSIBLE: SVGs are specifically designed for uploading and cutting with clean, editable layers. These are the best files to use with Cricut Design Space.

3

DO NOT USE PDF FILES: Cricut Design Space cannot upload PDFs directly. PDFs must be converted to SVG or PNG first. Some conversions lose detail or merge layers. Fonts may turn into outlines or even disappear entirely.

4

DXF FILE ISSUES: DXF files can work in Cricut Design Space, but with limitations. They only work on the Desktop app and won't upload on mobile. They often lose sizing or layer organization and may need extra setup.

MAT LOADED CROOKED

A crooked mat leads to crooked cuts. This cheat sheet helps you load your mat straight every time, with no wasted materials.

1

ALIGN THE MAT WITH THE LOADING GUIDES: Do not eyeball alignment. Use the raised guides built into both sides of the machine.

2

HOLD BOTH SIDES OF THE MAT EVENLY: Uneven pressure causes crooked loading. Keep your hands balanced and feed the mat in evenly.

3

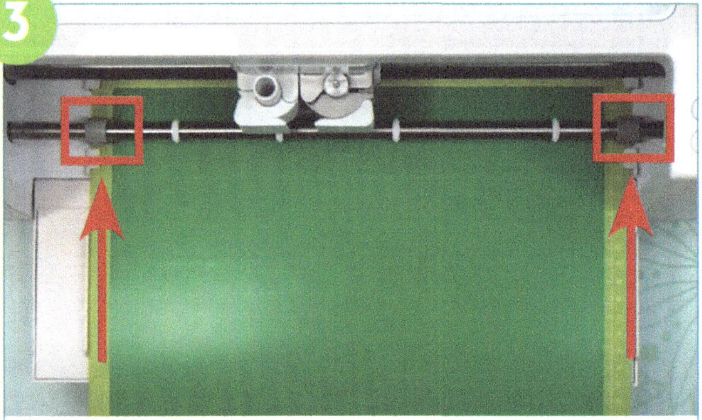

LET THE ROLLERS GRAB NATURALLY: Do not force the mat inward. Let the machine pull the mat in on its own.

4

UNLOAD AND RELOAD IF ALIGNMENT LOOKS OFF: It's better to unload and reload your mat than waste materials. Press the Load/Unload button on your machine or follow the prompts in Design Space if you are using a Joy or Joy Xtra.

CANVAS GRID TURNED OFF OR ON

The grid is one of Design Space's most useful tools when you know how to use it. This guide shows when to turn it on, off, and zoom for accuracy.

1

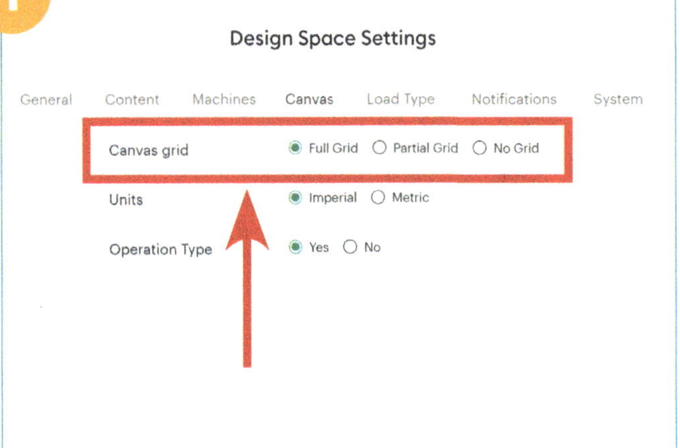

CHECK THE SETTING IN DESIGN SPACE SETTINGS: Click your name, then click "Settings," then "Canvas" within the Canvas menu. See if "Full Grid," "Partial Grid," or "No Grid" is selected.

2

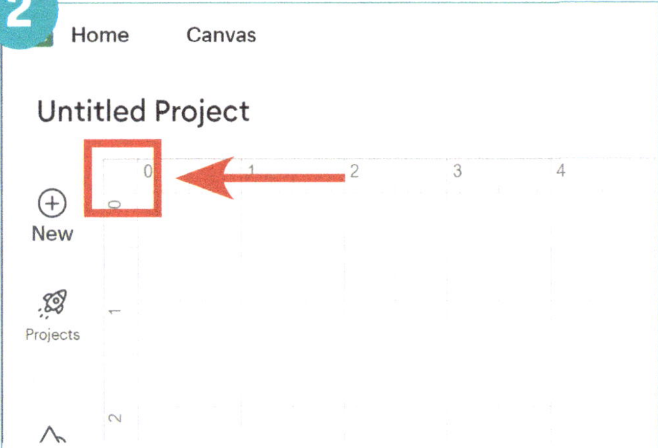

CLICK THE SQUARE IN THE TOP LEFT CORNER: Click the blank square in the top left corner between the vertical and horizontal rulers to toggle between grid settings.

3

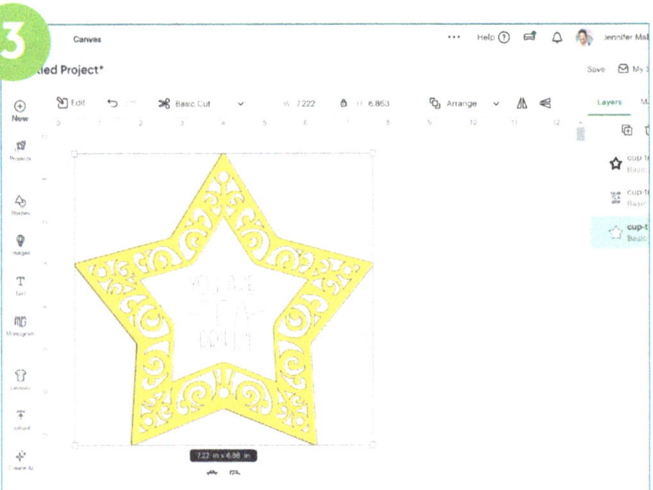

TURN THE GRID BACK ON FOR ALIGNMENT HELP: The grid helps visualize spacing and size. It's a critical reference tool.

4

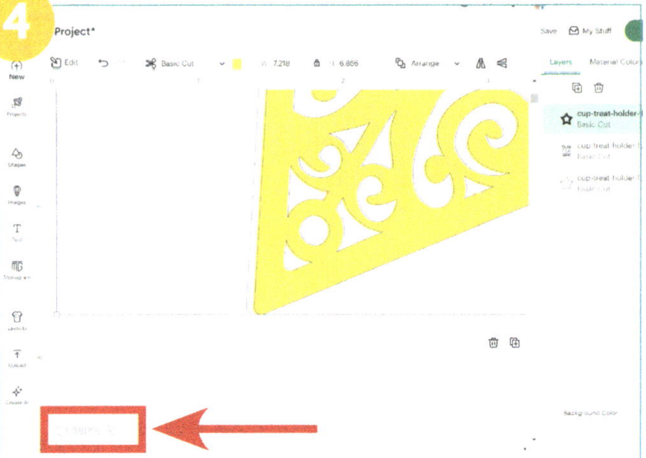

ZOOM IN TO CONFIRM ACCURATE SIZING: Grid lines help confirm the scale of your design. Zooming improves precision.

CANVAS UNITS CONFUSION

Switching between inches and millimeters can cause big mistakes. This cheat sheet helps you stay consistent and verify final dimensions.

1

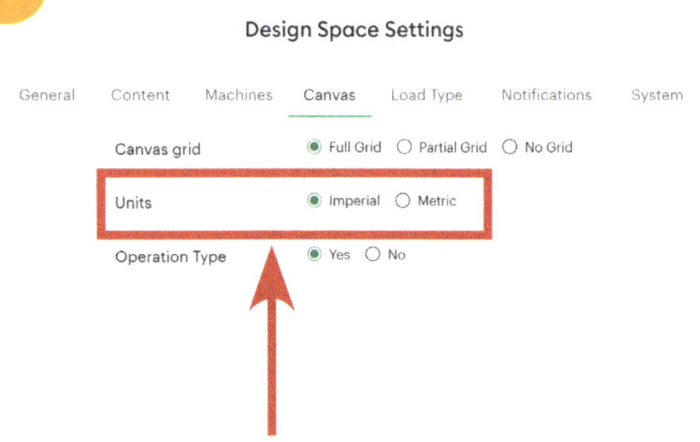

CHECK THE UNIT SETTING IN DESIGN SPACE SETTINGS: Click your name, then click "Settings," then "Canvas" within the Canvas menu. See if "Imperial" or "Metric" selected.

2

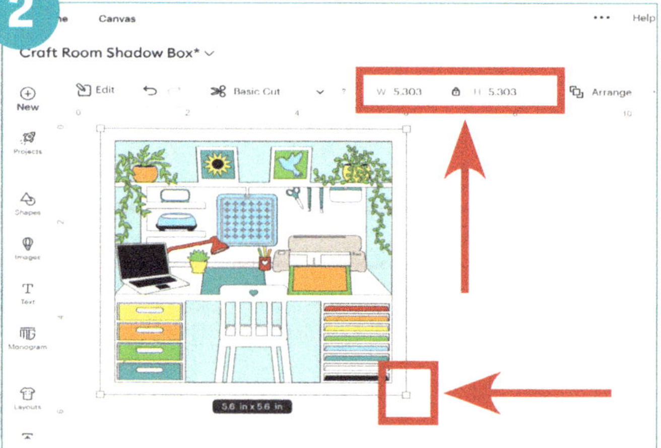

RESIZE DESIGNS AFTER CHANGING UNITS: Changing units does not resize existing designs. Adjust the size of the design manually with the resize handles or Height and Width boxes.

3

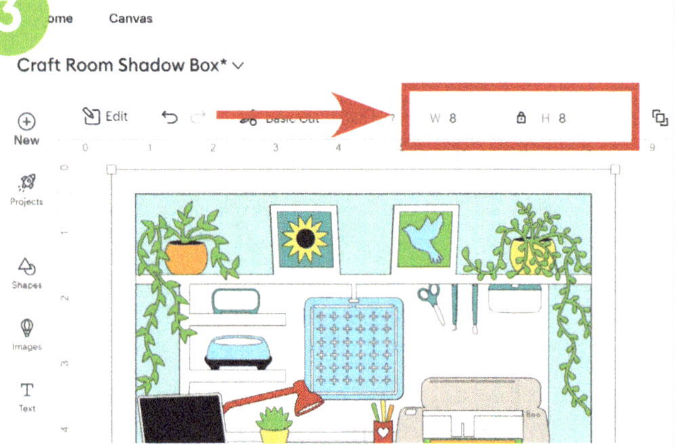

VERIFY FINAL DIMENSIONS CAREFULLY: Always confirm the finished size of your design using the Height and Width boxes. Small unit errors cause big mistakes.

4

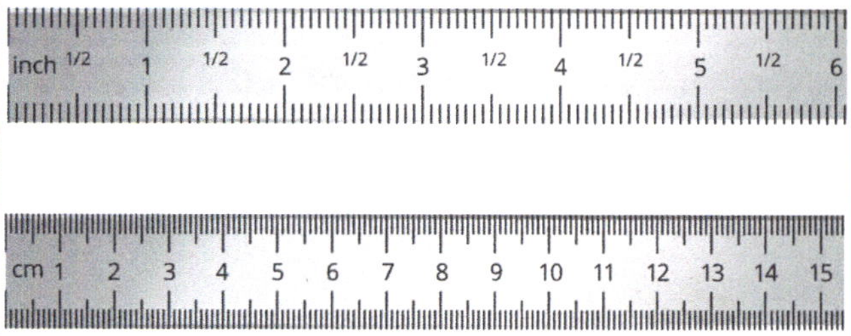

STICK TO ONE UNIT SYSTEM CONSISTENTLY: Consistency reduces confusion. Choose whichever unit system you're comfortable with.

GETTING CHARGED FOR ELEMENTS WITH ACCESS

Accidental charges happen fast if you're not watching closely. This guide shows how to spot paid elements before clicking Make.

1

LOOK FOR THE CRICUT ACCESS "A" ICON: This icon indicates included elements. The absence of this icon means an additional cost, especially for licensed elements.

2

WATCH FOR PRICE TAGS ON ELEMENTS: Prices indicate paid content, especially for licensed elements. Always verify if there's a cost before using an element.

3

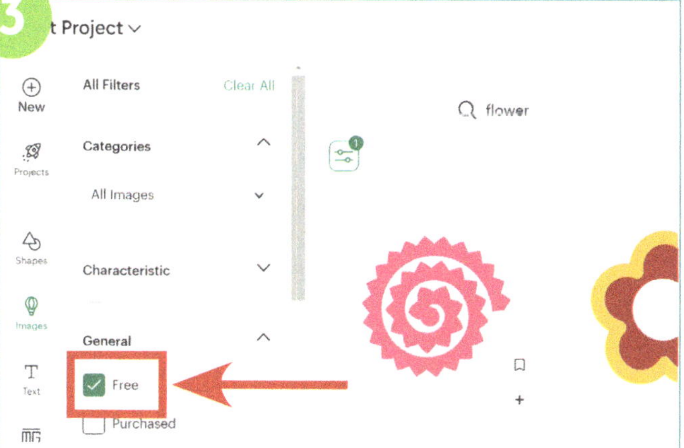

FILTER RESULTS TO FREE: Filtering prevents accidental charges. This is the safest option if you don't have a Cricut Access subscription.

4

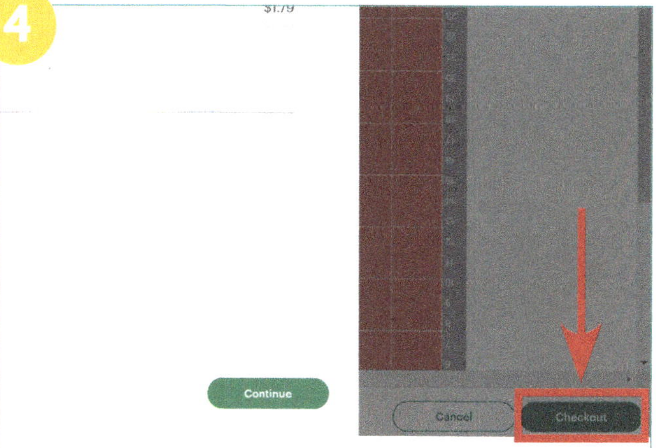

CONFIRM BEFORE CLICKING MAKE: Charges occur when cutting your design out. You will be prompted with a "Checkout" button and then pop-up once you click "Make."

WHICH ONE SHOULD I USE: FLATTEN, ATTACH, OR WELD?

Flatten, Attach, and Weld all change how your design behaves, but they do very different things. Using the wrong one can cause unexpected cuts or slow processing. This cheat sheet helps you choose the right option for the job.

1

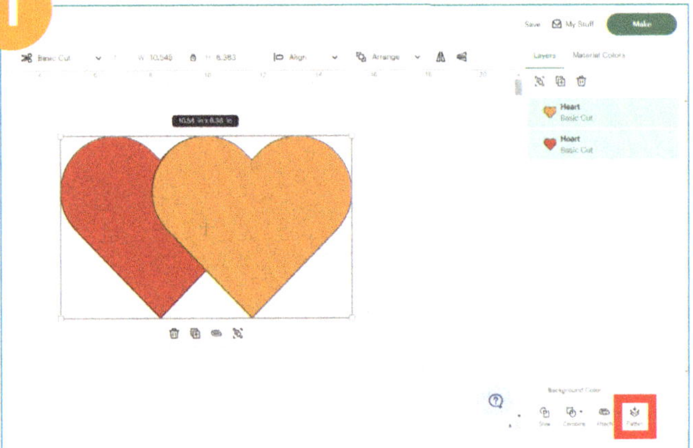

USE FLATTEN FOR PRINT THEN CUT: Flatten turns multiple layers into a single printable image. Use it anytime you want to print an image and then cut around it.

2

USE WELD TO MAKE ONE SOLID CUT: Weld permanently combines overlapping shapes into one piece. Use it when shapes should cut as a single object with no inner cut lines.

3

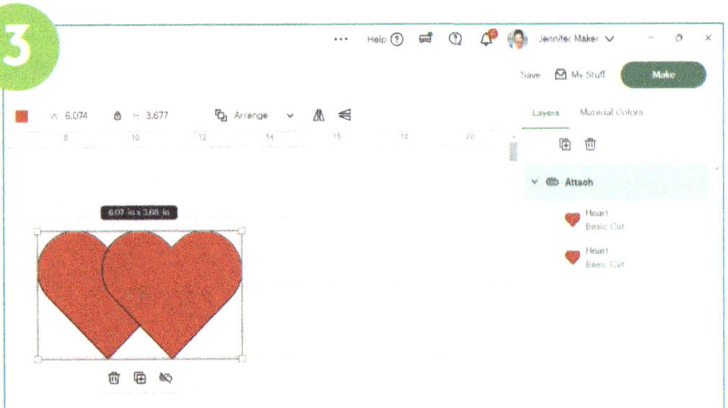

USE ATTACH TO CONTROL PLACEMENT: Attach keeps items in the same position on the mat but still cuts each shape separately. Use it when placement matters, like labels or layered designs.

4

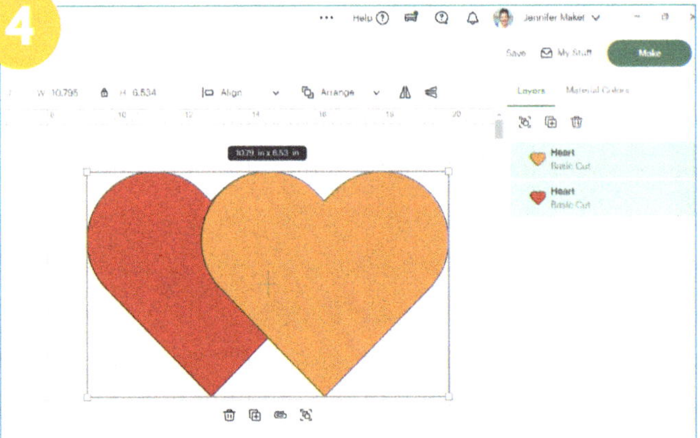

AVOID USING THESE INTERCHANGEABLY: Flatten, Attach, and Weld are not interchangeable. If your result looks wrong, undo and choose the option that matches your goal. Remember, Weld can only be undone in the current session.

GROUPING WHEN ATTACH IS NEEDED

Group and Attach are not interchangeable, and mixing them up changes your cut layout. This cheat sheet explains when placement truly matters.

1

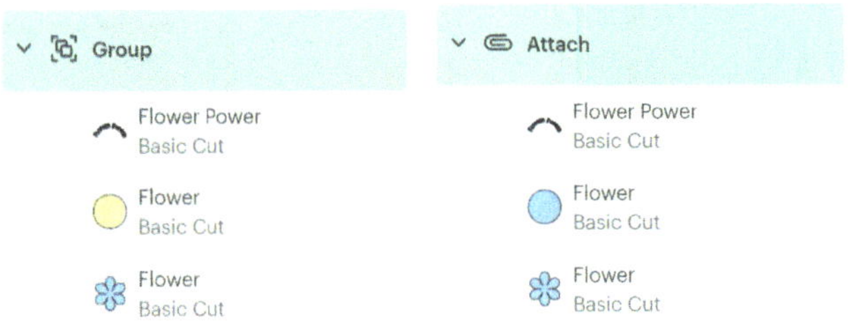

UNDERSTAND THE DIFFERENCE BETWEEN GROUP AND ATTACH: Group organizes items visually on the Canvas, but does nothing for cut placement. Attach controls cut placement.

2

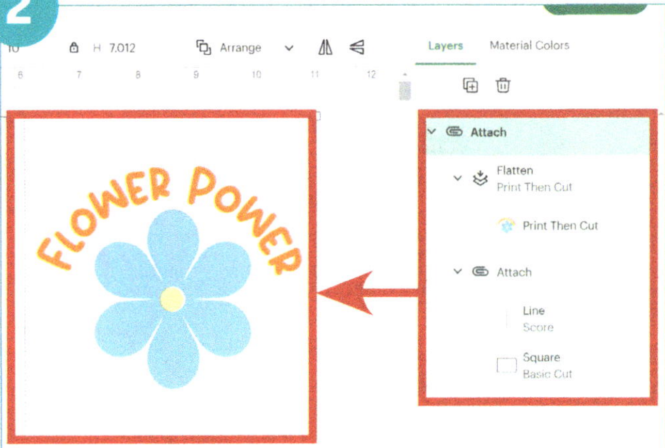

USE ATTACH WHENEVER PLACEMENT MATTERS: Text, labels, score lines, and Print Then Cut designs require use of the Attach tool in certain circumstances. Group is not the right tool.

3

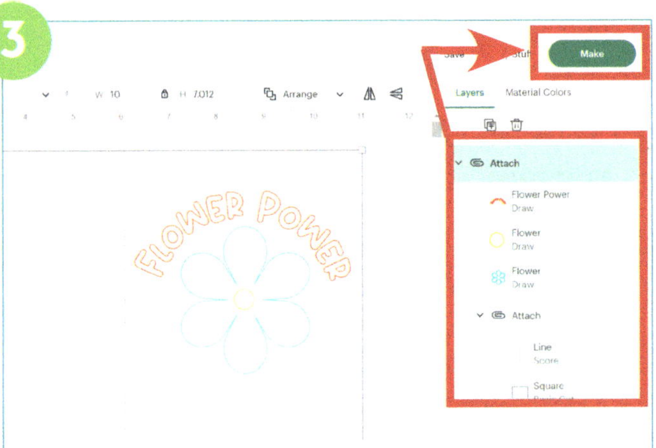

ATTACH ELEMENTS BEFORE CLICKING MAKE: Attach only works on the Canvas. It's too late to do it during the "Make" process. Go back to the Canvas to Attach.

4

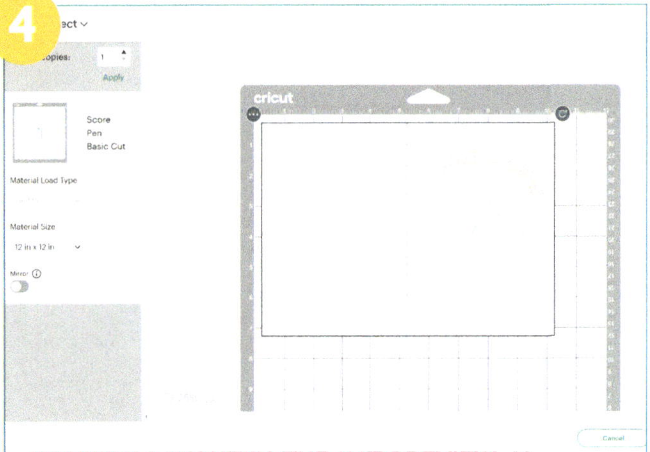

CONFIRM LAYOUT IN THE MAT PREVIEW: Your mat preview should match the Canvas exactly. If not, Attach is missing. Go back to the Canvas and Attach the elements to cut together.

FLATTENING WHEN ATTACH IS NEEDED

Flattening removes cut paths, which can be a problem for basic cuts. This guide helps you recognize when Flatten is the wrong tool.

1

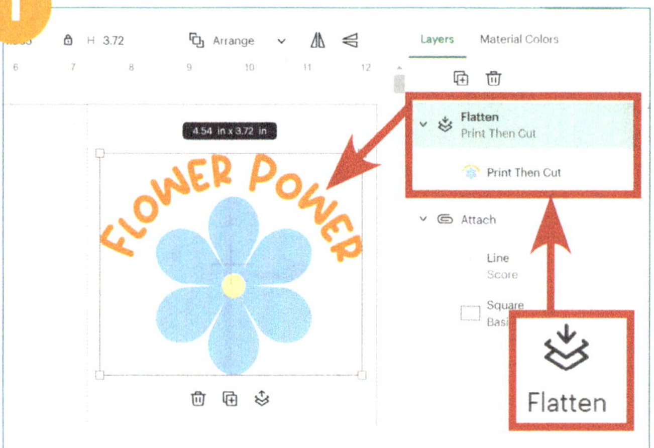

KNOW THAT FLATTEN CREATES PRINT THEN CUT IMAGES: Flatten removes cut paths. This changes how designs behave.

2

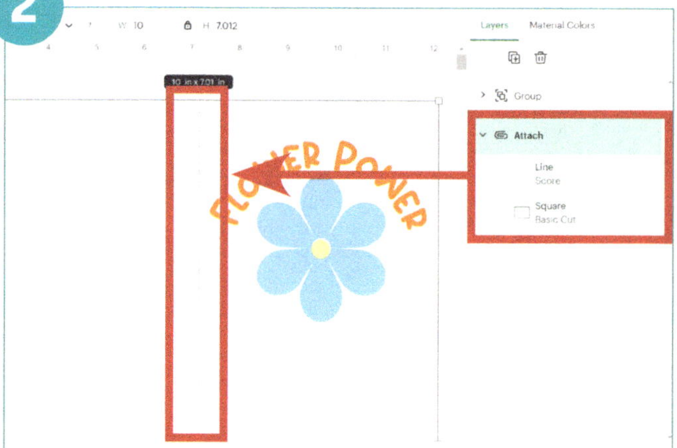

USE ATTACH FOR BASIC CUT PLACEMENT INSTEAD: Attach preserves cut lines. Flatten will cut the design as a single image. For example, always Attach score lines to an element.

3

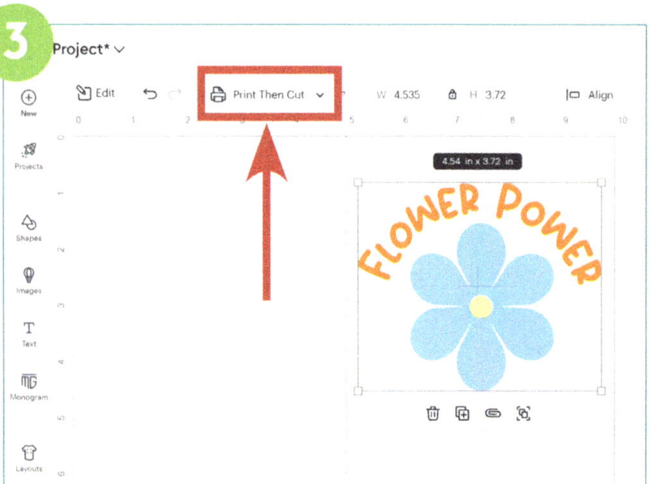

CHECK OPERATION TYPES AFTER FLATTENING: Flatten changes layers to printable instead of cuttable. Verify the action before cutting.

4

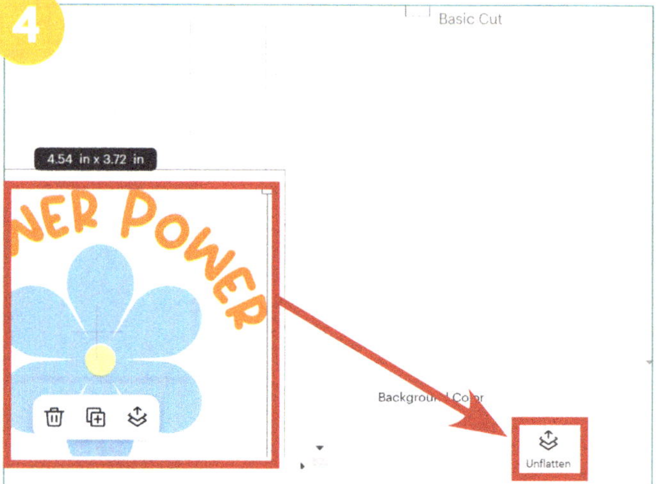

UNDO FLATTENING IF CUT OPTIONS DISAPPEAR: Missing cut options are a warning sign. Select the flattened image, then click "Unflatten."

ATTACHING WHEN FLATTEN IS NEEDED

Print Then Cut projects require Flatten, not Attach. This cheat sheet helps you avoid accidentally cutting everything apart.

1

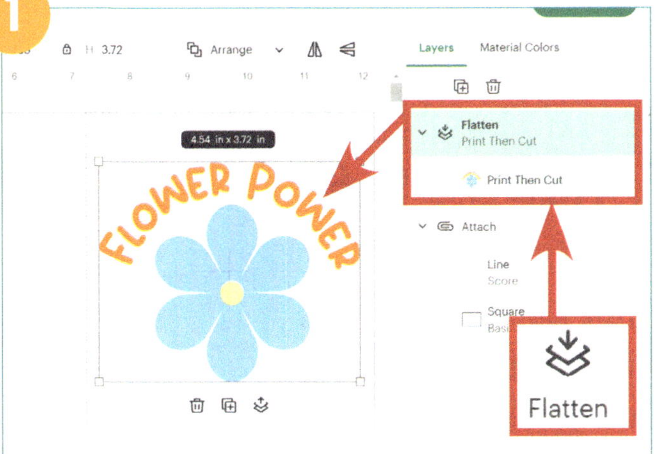

USE FLATTEN FOR PRINT THEN CUT DESIGNS: Flatten combines layers into a single printable image. Attach does not do this and instead cuts each element separately.

2

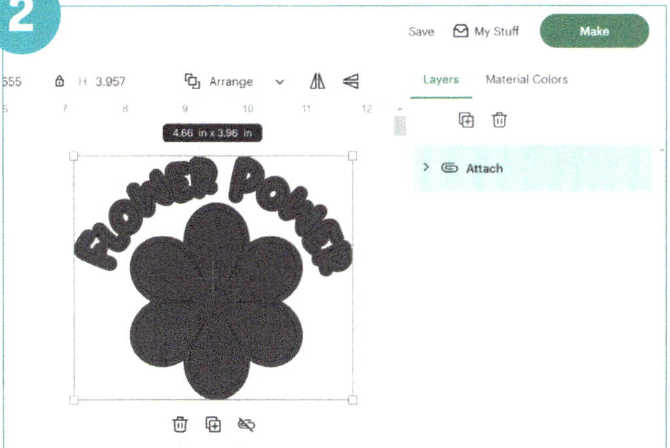

UNDERSTAND THAT ATTACH PRESERVES CUT PATHS: Attach is for cutting, not printing. If you Attach, all of the elements you have selected will turn the same color.

3

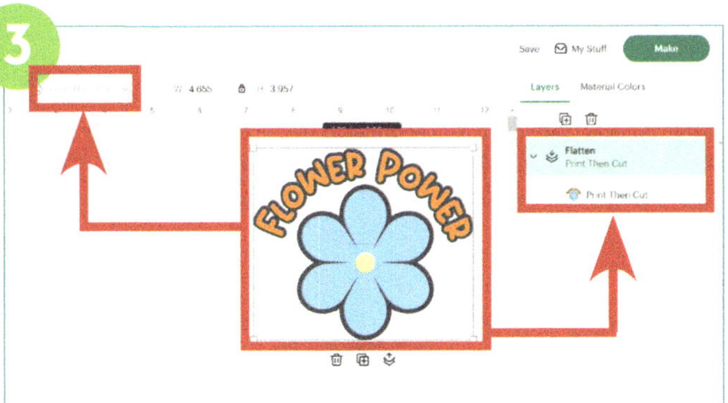

CHECK THE OPERATION TYPE CAREFULLY: Print Then Cut versus Cut determines behavior. Always verify the operation you are using.

4

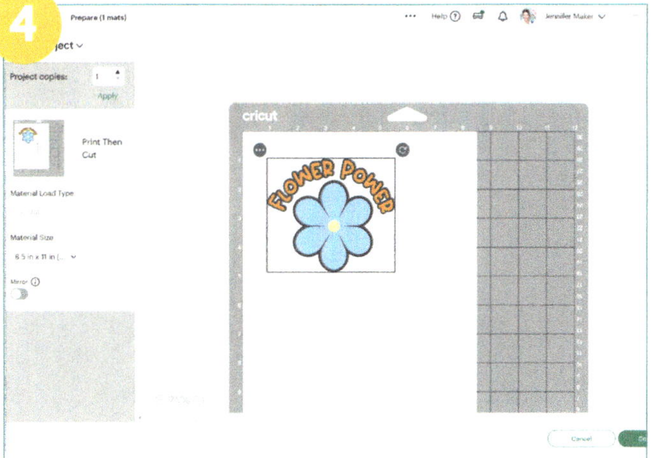

PREVIEW THE PRINT SCREEN BEFORE PROCEEDING: Preview confirms the correct setup. Never skip this step.

CRICUT SURVIVAL GUIDE

RESET, REBOOT, RECOVER

- Clearing Your Cache
- Reinstalling Design Space
- Logging Out vs Reinstalling Design Space
- When Firmware Causes Issues
- Safe Reset Steps

CLEARING YOUR CACHE

Corrupted cache files can cause all kinds of weird behavior. This guide walks you through safely clearing them before reinstalling anything.

1

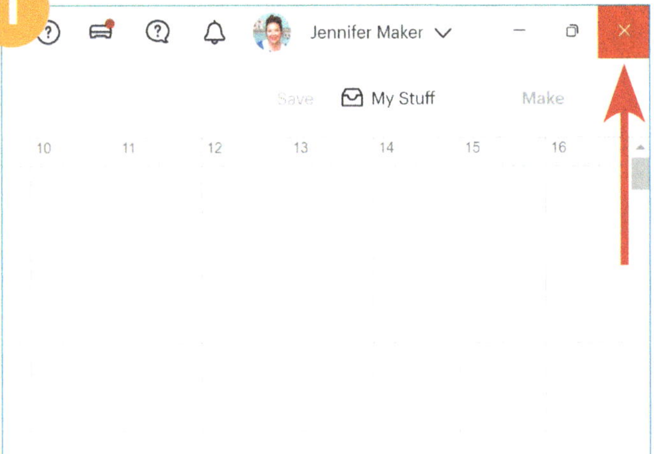

CLOSE DESIGN SPACE COMPLETELY: Minimizing is not enough. It must be fully closed, so click the X in the top right corner of the screen (top left corner for Macs) to close out of the program.

2

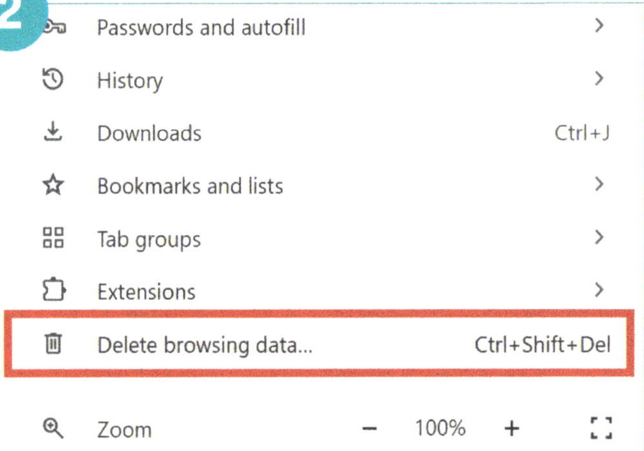

CLEAR THE CACHE: Clearing the cache deletes temporary files that could be causing problems. In the Chrome browser, click the three dots in the top right corner to find the menu.

3

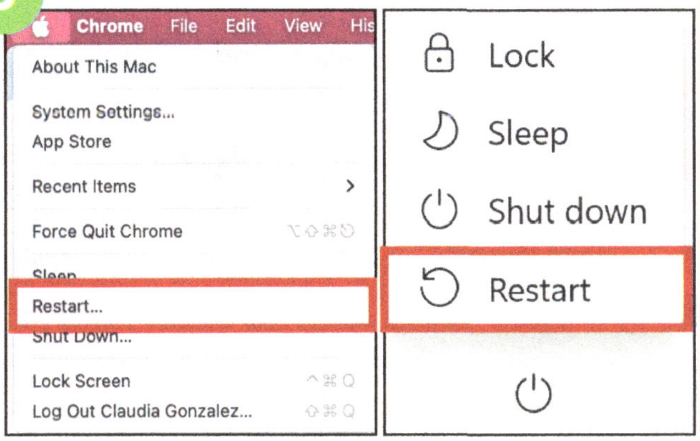

RESTART YOUR COMPUTER: This ensures changes take effect. Skipping restart reduces effectiveness and can leave programs running in the background.

4

REOPEN DESIGN SPACE AND TEST: Test your current version of Design Space before uninstalling and reinstalling the program. Cache clearing often solves issues.

REINSTALLING DESIGN SPACE

Sometimes a fresh install is the cleanest fix. This cheat sheet shows how to uninstall and reinstall Design Space the right way.

1

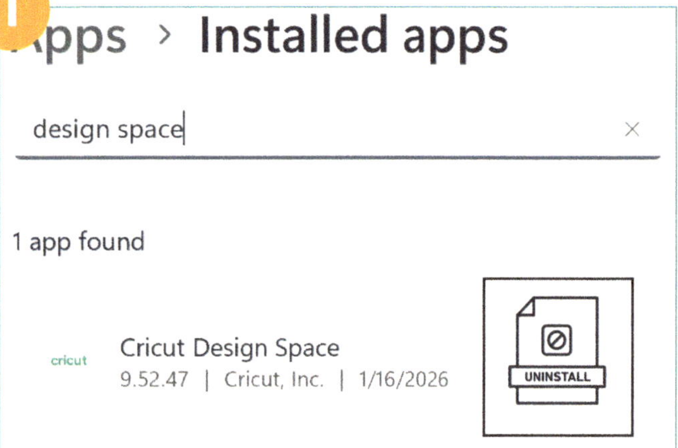

UNINSTALL DESIGN SPACE FULLY: For Macs, drag the Design Space icon to the Trash icon, then delete the trash. For Windows, go to "Add or Remove Programs" in the Settings menu.

2

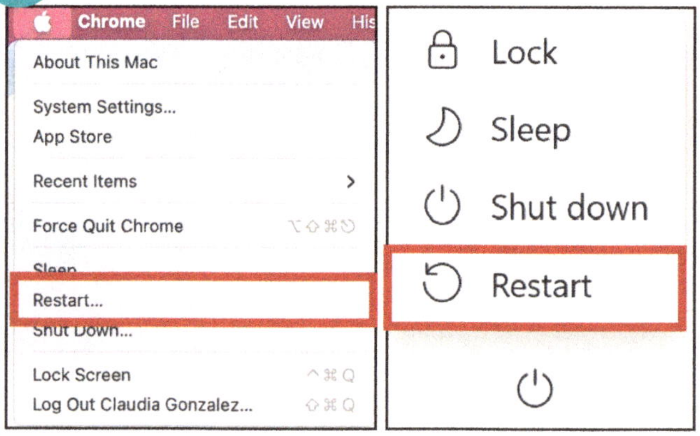

RESTART THE COMPUTER: This clears lingering processes that may be running in the background. It's a critical step, so don't skip it.

3

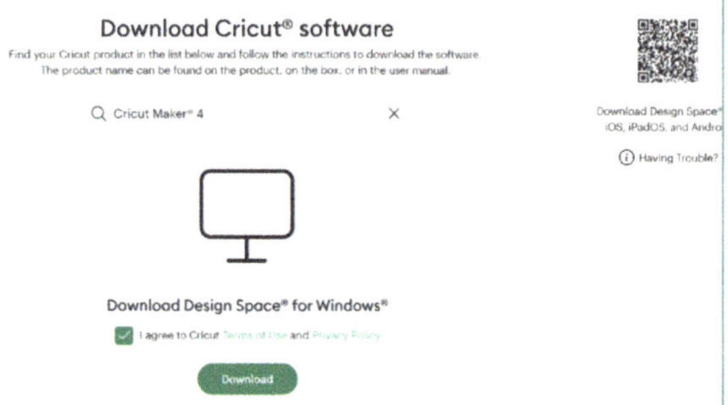

REINSTALL DESIGN SPACE: Avoid using old files. Fresh installs reduce errors, so go to design.cricut.com to download a fresh copy of Design Space.

4

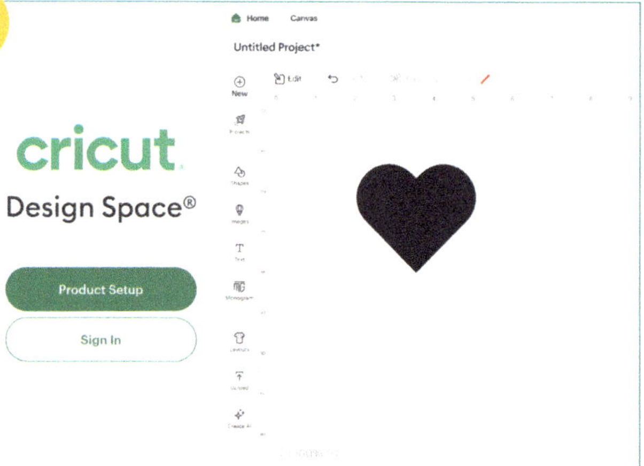

SIGN IN AND TEST BEFORE LOADING PROJECTS: After reinstalling Design Space, sign in and confirm stability by cutting a simple test project. Then resume work on your designs.

LOGGING OUT VS REINSTALLING DESIGN SPACE

Not every issue requires a full reinstall. This guide helps you choose the least disruptive fix first.

1

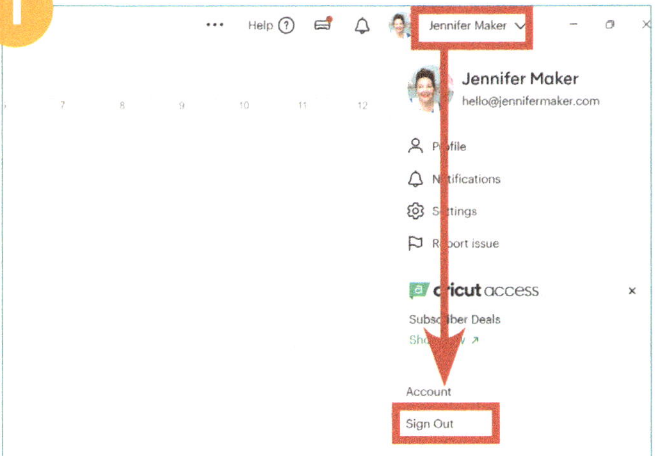

LOG OUT TO FIX SYNCING ISSUES: Logging out of Design Space by clicking your name, then "Sign Out," and then logging back in refreshes account data. It's a quick fix.

2

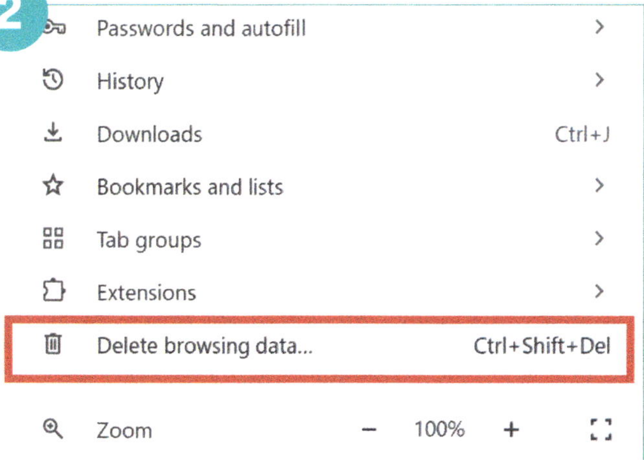

CLEAR CACHE IF LOGGING OUT DOESN'T HELP: Cache issues often mimic sync problems. Clear your cache as the next step.

3

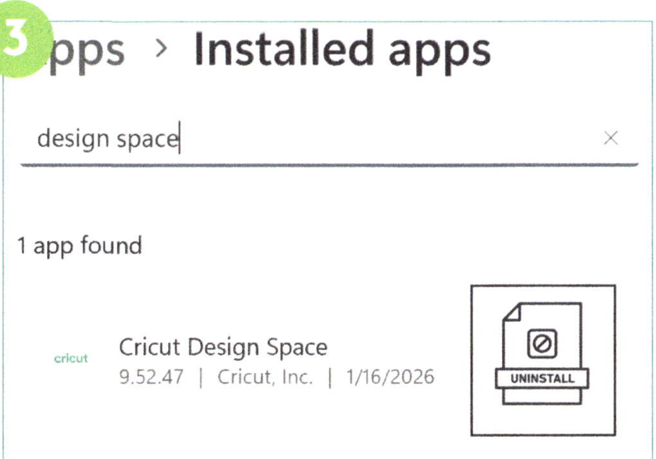

UNINSTALL FOR CRASHES OR FREEZING: Uninstalling Design Space resets everything. Use it for serious issues.

4

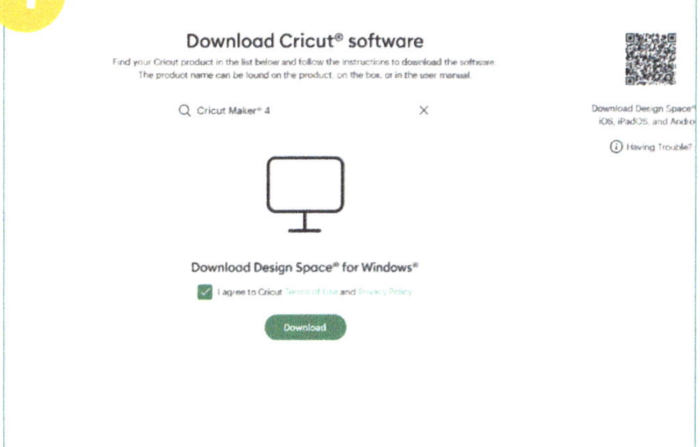

REINSTALL ONLY AS A LAST RESORT: Most problems resolve before reaching this step, so save reinstalling for persistent issues. Go to design.cricut.com.

WHEN FIRMWARE CAUSES ISSUES

Firmware updates can occasionally introduce problems. This cheat sheet helps you identify firmware-related issues and recover safely.

1

SEE IF PROBLEMS STARTED AFTER AN UPDATE: Sudden changes often indicate firmware issues. If you suspect that this is the issue, wait 24-48 hours for Cricut to fix bugs and glitches.

2

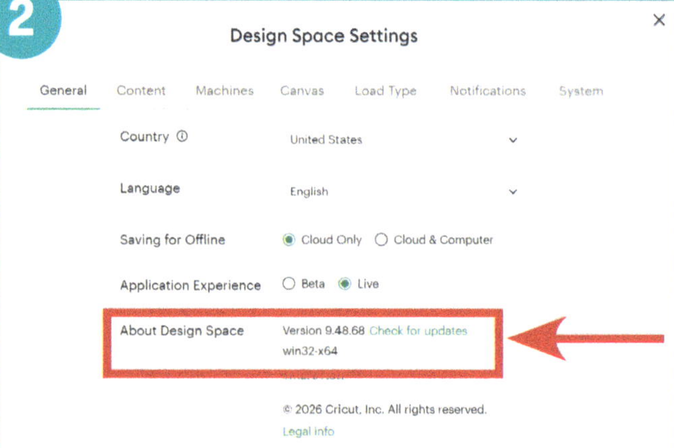

CHECK FIRMWARE STATUS IN DESIGN SPACE: Outdated firmware can cause instability. Verify that the version you are using is the most current version by clicking your name, then "Settings," and "Check for Updates."

3

RESTART YOUR CRICUT MACHINE: Power-cycling your Cricut refreshes firmware connections, so turn your Cricut off and back on again after 30-60 seconds. Always try this first.

4

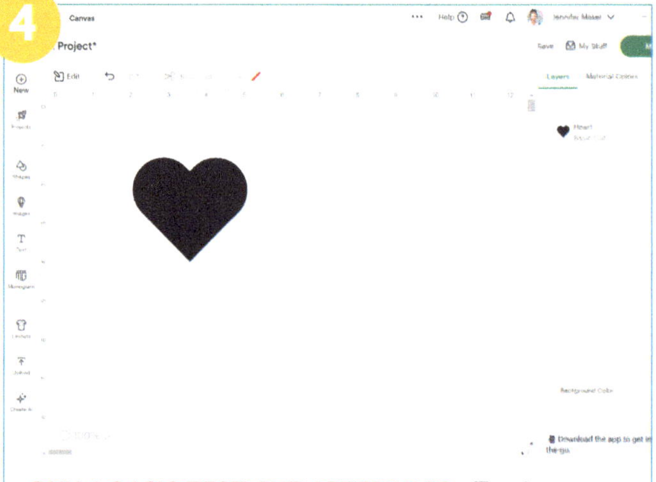

RUN A BASIC TEST CUT AFTERWARD: Testing a quick and simple project in Design Space confirms stability. Always verify that everything works correctly before resuming full projects.

SAFE RESET STEPS

A proper reset clears lingering power and communication issues. Follow these steps to reset your Cricut without risking damage.

1

POWER OFF AND UNPLUG THE MACHINE: Power off and fully unplug your Cricut. This stops all internal activity. It prepares the machine for reset.

2

WAIT AT LEAST 60 SECONDS: Time allows residual power to clear, so wait at least 60 seconds before plugging the machine back in and powering it on. Rushing reduces effectiveness.

3

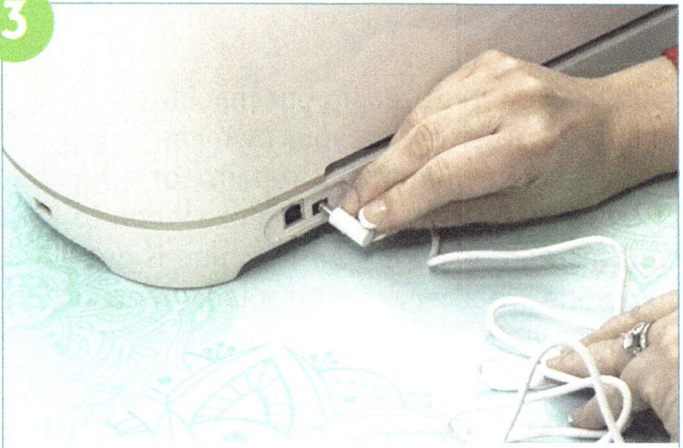

PLUG THE MACHINE BACK IN SECURELY: Ensure tight connections both with the cable and Cricut and the cable and power source. Loose cables cause repeat issues.

4

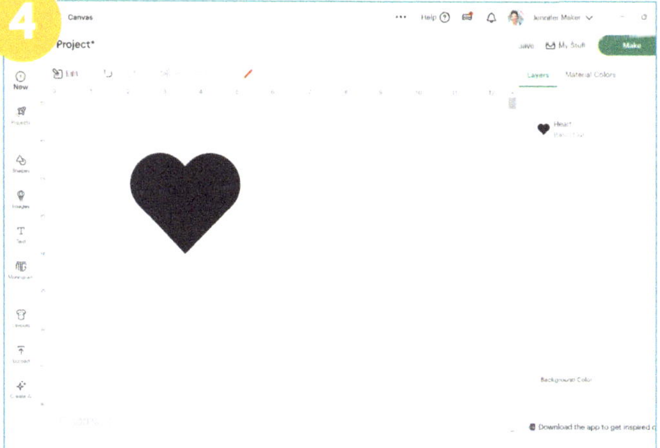

RESTART DESIGN SPACE AND TEST CUT: Testing a simple project in Design Space confirms stability. Always verify that everything works correctly before resuming full projects.

WHEN TO STOP TROUBLESHOOTING

At some point in every Cricut journey, there comes a moment when the most powerful troubleshooting step is knowing when to stop. This section exists to give you **permission to pause, step back, and recognize** when you've done enough. Not every problem can, or should, be solved with one more reboot, one more reinstall, or one more test cut. Part of becoming a confident Cricut user is learning to tell the difference between a fixable hiccup and a true hardware issue.

So how do you know when it's no longer "just a setting"? There are **clear signs** that point to hardware trouble, not user error. If your machine won't power on at all, freezes repeatedly mid-cut across multiple projects, makes loud grinding or slamming noises, fails to recognize tools no matter what you try, or behaves the same way after resets, firmware updates, and different materials – that's your signal. When problems persist across Design Space updates, different devices, and both USB and Bluetooth connections, it's very unlikely that the issue is you or your file.

This is also the point **where contacting Cricut Support at help.cricut.com** becomes the smart next step, not a last resort. Support can check error logs you can't see, confirm known firmware issues, and help determine whether your machine qualifies for repair or replacement. Before reaching out, it helps to gather a few things: your machine model and serial number, a short description of what's happening, and a list of the steps you've already tried. That preparation not only saves time, it shows you've done your part and speeds up the process.

Warranty considerations matter more than many crafters realize. If your machine is **still under warranty,** continuing to troubleshoot aggressively on your own can sometimes do more harm than good. Certain disassemblies, unofficial repairs, or third-party modifications can void coverage. This section helps you recognize when to stop experimenting and protect your investment instead. Even if your machine is out of warranty, knowing why it's failing helps you decide whether repair, replacement, or an upgrade makes the most sense for your crafting style.

Most importantly, let's reframe stopping as a success, not a defeat. Choosing smart next steps might mean contacting support, borrowing a friend's machine to confirm the issue, or deciding it's time for a new Cricut altogether. Whatever the outcome, you're no longer stuck guessing. You've moved from frustration to clarity, and that's exactly what this Survival Guide is here to give you.

IF YOUR QUESTION ISN'T ANSWERED HERE

This Survival Guide is designed to cover **the most common Cricut issues,** the ones that cause the most frustration and can usually be fixed with the right steps. If you've worked through the relevant section and your issue still isn't resolved, it doesn't mean you did anything wrong.

Some problems fall **outside the scope of troubleshooting**, such as account-specific issues, hardware defects, or changes introduced by very recent updates. When that happens, the best next step is to contact Cricut Support directly, since they're the only ones who can access account details, warranties, and system-level fixes.

To contact Cricut Support, head to help.cricut.com and choose the option to Contact Support. You can reach them by chat or phone (1-877-727-4288), and chat is often the fastest way to get help for common issues. Before you reach out, make sure you're logged into the Cricut account connected to your machine so they can quickly pull up your details.

To ensure the smoothest and quickest support experience, gather **a few key pieces of information** ahead of time: your machine model and serial number, the email address on your Cricut account, your operating system and device type, and a clear description of what's happening (including any error messages). If possible, screenshots or short videos of the issue can be incredibly helpful.

Having this information ready helps Cricut Support diagnose the problem faster, so you can get back to crafting with confidence instead of frustration.

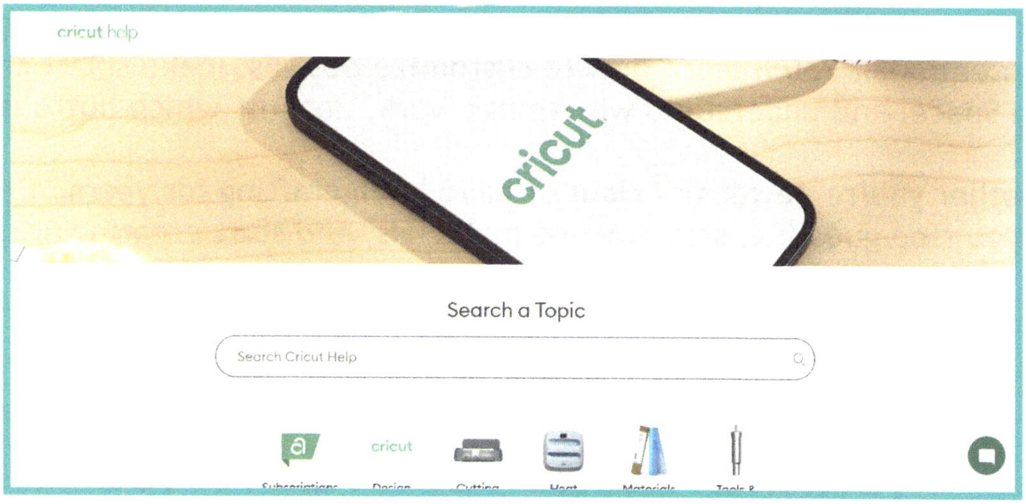

WHERE TO GO FROM HERE

ADVANCE WITH JENNIFERMAKER

If you enjoy making things but want to move beyond fixing issues and into designing with confidence, my ADVANCE program was created for you.

ADVANCE is where I teach you how to think like a designer and how to take ideas from your head and turn them into projects that feel personal, polished, and intentional. You'll learn how to customize designs, make smart choices in Design Space, and understand why things work, not just which buttons to click.

Whether you're newer to Cricut or have been crafting for years, ADVANCE helps you stop guessing, stop wasting materials, and start creating projects that feel truly your own.

Find out more at

jennifermaker.com/advance

CRAFT A LIFE YOU LOVE

Visit me at jennifermaker.com regularly for inspiration, help, and projects!

If you found yourself flipping through this Survival Guide to quickly solve a problem, the Cricut Coach Playbook works the same way, but for everyday Design Space tasks.

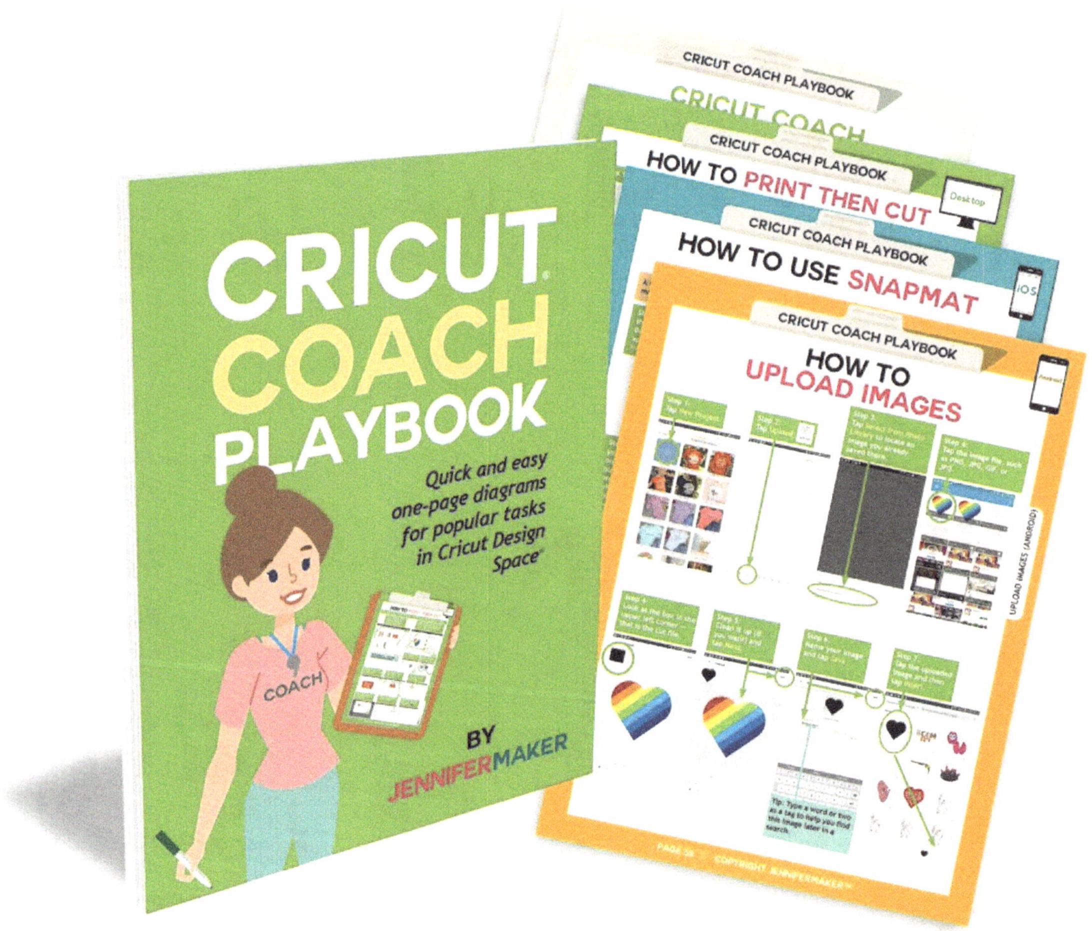

The Playbook is a visual reference you can keep open while you work, with clear, one-page diagrams that show you exactly where to click and what to do for common actions like uploading images, using SnapMat, and Print Then Cut. So you can stop searching and start making.

Find out more at

jennifermaker.com/cricutcoach

GO FROM HTV HASSLES TO HTV HAPPINESS WITH

HTV COOKBOOK!

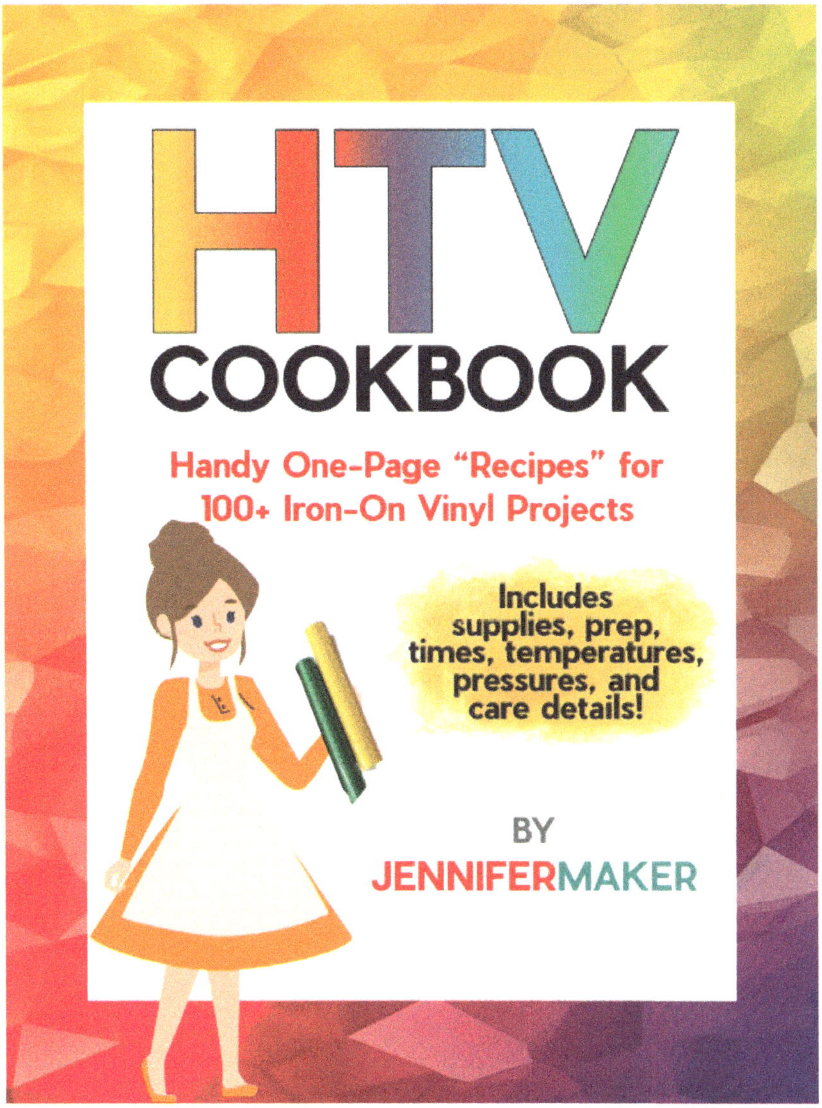

Find out more at

jennifermaker.com/htv-cookbook

Made in United States
Orlando, FL
04 November 2026

90202243R00063